I0645415

PLAYS & POEMS

THE INSATIATE COUNTESS

PRINCELYE PLEASURES
AT THE COURTE AT KENELWOORTH

RALPH ROYSTER DOYSTER

JOHN MARSTON

NICHOLAS UDALL

Published by Left of Brain Books

Copyright © 2021 Left of Brain Books

ISBN 978-1-396-31985-3

First Edition

All rights reserved. No part of this publication may be reproduced, distributed, or transmitted in any form or by any means, including photocopying, recording, or other electronic or mechanical methods, without the prior written permission of the publisher, except in the case of brief quotations embodied in critical reviews and certain other noncommercial uses permitted by copyright law. Left of Brain Books is a division of Left of Brain Onboarding Pty Ltd.

Table of Contents

JOHN MARSTON.

Of this Dramatist, scarcely any particulars are known; and the scanty information that has reached us, bears so apocryphal a character, that no dependance is to be placed upon its correctness. His biographer can do little more than lay before the reader the meagre and confused statement of Anthony Wood, who, in his "Athenæ Oxonienses," has the following passage:—

"John Marston, a Gentleman that wrote divers things of great ingenuity in the latter end of the Reign of Queen Elizabeth and beginning of King James I. did receive his academical education, as it seems, in Oxford, but in what House, unless in C. C. Coll. I cannot justly tell you. One John Marston, son of a father of both his names, of the City of Coventry, Esq. became either a Commoner, or a Gent. Com. Of Brasen-nose Coll. in 1591, and in the beginning of February 1593, he was admitted Bachelor of Arts, as the eldest son of an Esq.; and soon after completing this degree by determination, he went his way, and improved his learning in other faculties This person dying on the 24th of June, in 1634, was buried by his father, (some time a Counsellor of the Middle Temple,) in the Church belonging to the Temple, in the Suburb of London, under the stone which hath written on it OBLIVIONI SACRUM.

"Another John Marston I find to have been a Student in Corp. Ch. Coll. who was admitted Bachelor of Arts, 23rd of Feb. 1592, but in what County he was born, I cannot yet find, because, 1st. that he was not matriculated; 2nd. that he was not Scholar of that House, or Fellow; in the admissions of both which, their Counties of Nativity are constantly registered. This last of C. C. Coll. who seems to be John Marston, the Poet, (who died before 1633, *in which year most of his works were published by Will. Shakspeare*, and therefore cannot be that Marston of Brasen-nose College, who died in 1634, before 'tis told you, and has been taken by some of that House to be the same,) was not inferior to any, in writing of Comedies and Tragedies, especially if you consider the time when they were penned; and perhaps equal to some who lived twenty years after his time."

That Wood's account cannot be implicitly relied on, is shewn by the passage in Italics towards the conclusion of this extract; of which passage it need only be observed that in 1633; Shakspeare had been dead seventeen years. So satisfied, however, was Wood of his correctness, that after enumerating Marston's Works, he again says, "All his Plays, except two, were gathered together by Will. Shakspeare, the famous comedian, and, by his care, printed in London, 1633, 8vo."

It has been asserted though without any good authority, that upon quitting Oxford, Marston was entered of the Middle Temple, and afterwards chosen Lecturer of that Society. The opinion is founded upon a passage in Dugdale's "Origines," relative to a John Marston; but it remains to be proved that this was John Marston the Dramatist. In fact, as the said Lecturer was appointed to the office in the 34th year of Elizabeth's Reign, or 1592, it is plain enough that this could not have been either of the Marston's mentioned by Wood, the elder of whom only took the degree of B. A. in that year.

Oldys, in his M. S. additions to Langbaine, has surmised that Marston sprung from a family of the name, settled at Aftcot in Shropshire. It is farther said that, he married Mary, daughter of the Rev. W. Wikes, Chaplain to James the First, and Rector of St. Martin's, Wiltshire; and this is in some measure confirmed by what Ben Jonson told Drummond of Hawthornden, in his famous conversation with him, *viz.* that Marston wrote his father-in-law's Sermons, and his father-in-law, Marston's Dramas; adding, that he (Jonson) had often fought with Marston. What occupation Marston followed, or whether he supported himself solely by his writings for the Stage, it is now impossible to ascertain; but Wood asserts that "he was in great renown for his wit and ingenuity in 1606."

The time of his death is equally uncertain but it will be seen by the Dedication, which the bookseller prefixed to six of his plays printed in 1633, that he was then living. Oldys supposes that he died shortly after, aged about sixty years. Subjoined is a list of his Plays, with their several editions:—

 1. ANTONIO AND MELLIDA.—Hist. Play, 4to. 1602.
 2. ANTONIO'S REVENGE.—Trag. 4to. 1602. 3.
 3. HE MALCONTENT.—Trag. Com. 4to. 1604, (Two Editions.)
 4. THE DUTCH COURTEZAN.—Com. 4to. 1605.
 5. PARASITASTER; on, THE FAWN.—Com. 4to. 1606.

6. THE WONDER OF WOMAN; OR, SOPHONISBBA. Trag. 4to. 1606.[1]

7. WHAT YOU WILL.—Com. 4to. 1607.

8. THE INSATIATE COUNTESS.—Trag. 4to. 1613, 4to. 1631.

Of these, all but the, 3rd and 8th were printed in one volume, small 8vo. 1633, by a bookseller named William Sheares, whom Wood, has blunderingly transformed into William Shakspeare, the Dramatist, as shewn in the preceding extract from his Athenæ Oxonienses. What is still more curious, this ridiculous mistake was copied into Cibber's "Lives of the Poets," and Baker's "Companion to the Playhouse." To complete the collection of Marston's Works, the present volume has been undertaken, printed uniformly with that of 1633, which is now extremely scarce, and sells for a high price. A Dedication prefixed to Sheares's book, is here reprinted; as, owing to some accident, copies are seldom met with in which it occurs. Indeed, so rare is it, that the Editor of the Old English Plays, published in 1814–15, says he never could meet with a copy containing it.

In addition to the above Plays, Marston was author of

1. "The Metamorphosis of Pigmalion's Image, and Certain Satires, 1598."

2. "The Scourge of Villany. Three Books of Satires, 1599".

3. "The Argument of the Spectacle presented to the Sacred Majesties of Great Britain and Denmark, as they passed through London."—This is in M. S. in the British Museum.

He also joined with Chapman and Ben Jonson, in writing the, Comedy called "Eastward Hoe," 1605; a passage in which, reflecting on the Scots, gave so much offence, that the authors were committed to prison, and, as some have said, narrowly escaped losing their ears and noses. In the early part of his career, Marston made some attacks upon Jonson in his Satires; and having afterwards joined with Decker in ridiculing Ben's "Cynthia's Revels," they were' in return, satirised by him in his "Poetaster," 1601; under the names of

---

[1] Though not *printed* till 1606, this Tragedy appears to have been *acted* long before; since in the Account-Book of Henslowe, Proprietor of the Rose Theatre, given in Malone's "History of the Stage," there is a statement of the receipts on the 15th of October, 1595, "At the 'Wonder of a Woman.'"

Crispinus and *Demetrius*. Decker was the principal object of the satire; but some very happy strokes are also directed against Marston. His fondness for high-sounding, tumid phrases is pleasantly ridiculed; and the Prologue to "Antonio's Revenge," which' abounds with such, is particularly aimed at. The quarrel between Ben and Marston was not, however, of long duration, since it is evident that shortly after, they were living 1n habits of the closest intimacy and friendship. This is apparent, not only from the circumstances attendant upon the production of "Eastward Hoe," but from Marston's having in 1604 dedicated his "Malcontent" to Jonson, in terms expressive of high admiration, and having also prefixed a short complimentary poem to Jonson's "Sejanus," 1605. It has nevertheless been asserted by Langbaine, and from him heedlessly copied by other writers, that some remarks upon translations from the ancients, which occur in the Preface to "The Wonder of Women," 1606, were levelled at Jonson's "Catiline" and "Sejanus." That this is incorrect in one particular, is sufficiently proved by the fact that "Catiline" was not produced till 1611, five years alter the publication of "The Wonder of Women;" and they who consult the Preface in question, and observe the general nature of Marston's remarks, will feel no hesitation in admitting that it is not probable they were aimed at any particular individual.

Of Marston's character as a writer, Mr. Gifford speaks thus:—"His Dramatic Works are distinguished by nothing so much as, a perpetual bluster, an overstrained reaching after sublimity of expression, which ends in abrupt and, unintelligible starts, and bombast anomalies of language." (*Jonson's Works, Vol. 2, p.* 517.) There is some truth in the remark; but Mr. Gifford is by no means infallible; and his censure on this, as on many other occasions, is by far too sweeping and indiscriminate. A perusal of one or two of Marston's Plays will fully shew this; and it may safely be predicted, that the fans which has survived the lapse of two centuries, is not destined to fall before the attack of the modern Zoilus.

EPISTLE DEDICATORY.

(Prefixed by the Bookseller to the Edition of Marston's Plays,
printed in 1633.)

TO THE RIGHT HONOURABLE, THE LADY ELIZABETH CARIE, VISCOUNTESSE FAWKLAND.

Many opprobies and aspersions have not long since been cast upon Playes in generall,[2] and it were requisite and expedient that they were vindicated from them; but, I referre that taske to those whose leasure is greater, and learning more transcendent. Yet, for my part, I cannot perceive wherein they should appeare so vile and abominable, that they should bee so vehemently inveighed against. Is it because they are PLAYES? The name, it seemes, somewhat offends them; whereas, if they were styled WORKES, they might have their approbation also. I hope that I have now somewhat pacified that precise sect, by reducing all our Author's severall Playes into one volume;[3] and so stiled them THE WORKS OF MR. JOHN MARSTON, who was not inferiour unto any in this kinde of writing, in those dayes when these were penned; and, I am perswaded, equall unto the best poets of our times. If the lines bee not answerable to my encomium of him, yet herein beare with him, because they were his JUVENILIA and youthfull recreations. Howsoever, hee is free from all obscene speeches, which is the chiefe cause that makes Playes to bee so odious unto most men. Hee abhorres such writers, and their workes; and hath professed himselfe an enemie to all such as stuffe their scenes with ribaldry, and lard their lines with scurrilous taunts and jests; so that, whatsoever, even in the Spring of his yeeres, hee hath presented upon the private and publike

---

[2] Prynne's "Histrio-Mastix," which was published in 1633, is here alluded to.

[3] Mr. Sheares could scarcely be ignorant that he had *not* reprinted *all* his author's Play. He probably feared that he should render the volume too bulky, were he to include "The Insatiate Countess" and "The Malcontent."

Theater, now, in his Autumne and declining age, hee need not bee ashamed of. And, were it not that hee is so farre distant from this place, hee would have beene more carefull in revising the former impressions, and more circumspect about this, then I can. In his absence, Noble Lady, I have been imboldened to present these WORKES unto your Honour's view; and the rather, because your Honour is well acquainted with the Muses. In briefe, Fame hath given out, that your Honour is the mirror of your sex, the admiration, not onely of this Iland, but of all adjacent and dominions which are acquainted with vertues and endowments. If your Honour accept I, with my Booke, am ready prest and bound to be

Your truly devoted,
WILLIAM SHEARES.

THE INSATIATE COUNTESS

A

TRAGI-COMEDY,

JOHN MARSTON.

PROLEGOMENA.

It is fortunate for Marston's reputation as a Dramatist, that "The Insatiate Countess" cannot be cited as a fair specimen of his powers. Had he produced nothing of a superior description, his name would long since have been forgotten; or known only to those whose studies lie amongst "such reading as was never read." It was perhaps, his earliest production; or a hasty composition, intended to answer some occasional purpose.

Two old editions of the Play exist, then title-pages run thus:—

"The Insatiate Countesse, a Tragedie, acted at White-Fryers. Written by John Marston—London. Printed by T. S. for Thomas Archer, and are to be sold at his Shop in Pope's-head Pallace, neere the Royall Exchange. 1613." 4to.

"The Insatiate Countesse, a Tragedie, acted at White-Fryers. Written by John Marston.—London. Printed by I. N. for Hugh Perrie, and are to be sould at his Shop, at the signe of the Harron, in Brittaine's Burse. 1631." 4to.

Langbaine, however, mentions an edition dated so early as 1603. For this I have enquired most diligently, but to no purpose; and I am therefore strongly inclined to suspect that the date, 1603, in Langbaine's book, is an error of the press for 1613. Should this suspicion prove to be unfounded, I shall consider myself the most unfortunate of editors, in not having been able to meet with the *first* edition, which would doubtless have relieved me from a world of wearisome arid fruitless conjecture, in attempting to throw some light upon passages which, in the copies I possess, are terribly obscure. It would, I believe, be impossible to select from amongst the old editions of our early Plays, any, more thoroughly and ridiculously corrupt, than the quartos of "The Insatiate Countess," which were evidently printed from what Colman has styled "the most inaccurate and barbarous of all manuscripts, the Prompter's book." To those who are acquainted with the originals, it is unnecessary to remark farther upon this point; and, to those who never saw the quartos, it must be impossible to convey the slightest idea of the blunders which everywhere pervade them. The stage-directions are interwoven with the text; prose is printed as verse, and verse as prose; punctuation is completely disregarded; and the characters are continually confounded with one another, "in most admired disorder." I have endeavoured, by correcting these mistakes, to render the progress of the plot somewhat less confused, and trust that the attempt has not been wholly unsuccessful. A few Notes are appended, in the composition of which, brevity has been principally studied. I have not, as is too often the practice, "held my farthing candle to the sun," and insulted the understanding of the reader, by loading the page with explanations of passages in themselves sufficiently intelligible: though nothing can be more easy than such a display of reading, in this age of Indexes and Cyclopædias. The text of the old copies has been adhered to, as closely as possible; and it may, perhaps, be thought that I might have been less scrupulous in hazarding alterations, when the corrupt condition of the originals is remembered. Where, however, I have met with a passage hopelessly obscure, I have preferred laying it before the reader as I found it, to cutting the Gordian knot, by fanciful and capricious emendations. I of course except the removal of palpable typographical blunders, with which the old copies abound, and which I have in general silently corrected, without deeming it necessary to celebrate every instance of such wonderous acuteness, by a Note. A few only are pointed out, merely as specimens of the manner in which the author's meaning has been perverted, by carelessness or ignorance.

For the several personages in this Play, little interest is excited. The heroine is a truly disgusting wretch. Langbaine asserts that the character was intended for a covert satire upon Joan, Queen of Naples; though I believe he has "found in Homer what was never there," and imputed to Marston what he had not in his thoughts. Joan, 'tis true, married four husbands, and *Isabella*, it will be seen, has one husband and three paramours; but there the resemblance, such as it is, completely ends. Joan, with all her vices, was a woman of talent; whilst *Isabella* is a mere "remorseless, treacherous, lecherous, kindless" wanton, who spends her life in the commission of every crime, and terminates her career upon the scaffold, quibbling and cursing, an object of contempt and detestation. The remaining characters are too weakly sketched, for us to feel much interest about them. *Claridiana* and *Mizaldus* are a couple of pitiful fools, and their wives scarcely better than two strumpets. The indecency which pervades the comic portions of the dialogue, does Marston little honour, and forms a curious commentary upon that part of the Dedication prefixed to his Six Plays published in 1633, wherein the purity of his writings is commended. The reader will scarcely be surprised that few remarks have been wasted upon such disgusting ribaldry.

It is asserted in the "Biographia Dramatica," that Mr. Kemble possesses a copy of "The Insatiate Countess," having in the title-page the name of one William Barksted as the author; and Mr. Jones infers from hence, that it is probable the Play was not written by Marston. That this is too hasty a conclusion, will be admitted by all who are aware of the tricks that were played with title-pages two centuries ago; but, for the sake of Marston's memory, I am willing to believe that the Play was not entirely written by him, and that the comic parts were by this Barksted. If my conjecture be correct, it will account for the rejection of "The Insatiate Countess" and "The Malcontent," when Marston's other works were collected in 1633; (*Vide Note 3*, p. 5)The bookseller intending to print the Plays only which were *wholly* written by his author, of course omitted those in which he was assisted by Barksted and Webster.

DRAMATIS PERSONÆ.

AMAGO, *Duke of Venice.*
DUKE of MEDINA.
MENDOSA FOSCARII, *Nephew to Amago.*
ROBERTO, *Count of Cyprus.*
ROGERO, *Count of Arsena.*
GNIACA, *Count of Gaza.*
GUIDO, *Friend of Roberto and Rogero.*
TWO CARDINALS.
DON SAGO, *A Spanish Colonel.*
CLARIDIANA, *Venetian Citizen.*
MIZALDUS, *Venetian Citizen.*
A PAGE.
ISABELLA, *Countess of Suevia.*
LADY LENTULUS, *A Young Widow.*
ABIGAIL, *Wife to Claridiana.*
THAIS, *Wife to Mizaldus.*
ANNA, *An Attendant upon Isabella.*

*Senators, Officers, Lieutenant, Captain of the Watch, Watchmen, Soldiers,
Servants, Friar, Executioner.*

SCENE.—*During the First and Second Acts, at* VENICE; *afterwards,
occasionally at* PAVIA.

ACT I.

SCENE 1.—*Venice.*—*A Chamber.*—*The* Countess of Suevia, *discovered sitting at a Table covered with black, on which stand two, black Tapers, lighted: she in Mourning.*

Enter ROBERTO, ROGERO, *and* GUIDO.

Guido. What should we do in this Countess's dark hole? She's sullenly retired, as the turtle; every day has been a black day with her, since her husband died; and what should we unruly members make here?

Rog. As melancholy night masks up heaven's face,
So doth the Ev'ning Star present herself
Unto the careful shepherd's gladsome eyes,
By which unto the fold he leads his flock.

Guido. Zounds, what a sheepish beginning is here! 'Tis said, true love is simple; and it may well hold; and thou art a simple lover.

Rob. See, how yon star, like beauty in a cloud,
Illumines darkness, and beguiles the Moon
Of all her glory in the firmament.

Guido. Well said, Man i'the Moon! Was ever such astronomers! Marry, I fear none of these will fall into the right ditch.[4]

Rob. Madam.

Countess. Ha, Anna! what, are my doors unbarr'd?

Guido. I'll assure you, the way into your ladyship is open.

Rob. And, God defend that any prophane hand
Should offer sacrilege to such a Saint!
Lovely Isabella, by this duteous kiss,
That draws part of my soul along with it,
Had I but thought my rude intrusion
Had wak'd the dove-like spleen harbour'd within you,
Life and my first-born should not satisfy

---

[4] There appears to be an allusion to some Proverb here, but I am not sufficiently versed in such lore, to be able to explain it.

Such a transgression, worthy of a check!
But, that immortals wink at my offence,
Makes me presume more boldly. I am come
To raise you from this so infernal sadness.

    Countess. My lord of Cyprus, do not mock my grief,
Tears are as due a tribute to the dead,[5]
As fear to God, and duty unto Kings,
Love to the just, or hate unto the wicked.

    Rob. Surcease!
Believe, it is a wrong unto the gods;
They sail against the wind, that wail the dead;
And, since his heart hath wrestled with death's pangs,
From whose stern cave none tracts[6] a backward path,
Leave to lament this necessary change,
And thank the gods, for they can give as good.

    Countess. I wail his loss! sink him ten cubits deeper,
I may not fear his resurrection!
I will be sworn upon the holy writ,
I mourn thus fervent, 'cause he died no sooner.
He buried me alive,
And mew'd me up, like Cretan Dædalus;
And with wall-ey'd jealousy kept me from hope
Of any waxen wings to fly to pleasure;
But now his soul her Argus' eyes hath clos'd,
And I am free as air. You of my sex,
In the first flow of youth, use you the sweets
Due to your proper beauties; ere the ebb
And long wane of unwelcome change shall come!
Fair women play; she's chaste whom none will have.—
(*Aside.*) Here is a man of a most mild aspéct,
Temp'rate, effeminate,[7] and worthy love,

---

    [5] The 4to. 1631, reads—

                "Tears are as due, as tribute to the dead."

    [6] *Tract* and *track* seem formerly to have been synonimous.

    [7] Effeminate was occasionally used for polite or accomplished by our old writers.

One that with burning ardour hath pursued me;
A donative he hath of ev'ry god;
Apollo gave him locks; Jove his high front;
The God of Eloquence, his flowing speech;
The feminine deities strow'd all their bounties
And beauty on his face: that eye was Juno's;
Those lips were hers[8] that won the golden ball;
That virgin-blush, Diana's; here they meet,
As in a sacred synod.—My lords, I must entreat,
Awhile, your wish'd forbearance.
    Omnes. We obey you, lady.

[Exeunt Rogero and Guido.

    Countess. (*To Roberto.*) My lord, with you I'd have some conference.
I pray, my lord, do you woo ev'ry lady
In this phrase you do me?
    Rob. Fairest, till now,
Love was an infant in my oratory.
    Countess. And kiss thus, too?   [*Kisses him.*
    Rob. I never was so kiss'd; leave thus to please;
Flames into flames, seas thou pour'st into seas.
    Countess. Pray frown, my lord; let me see how many wives
You'll have.[9] Heigh-ho! you'll bury me, I see.
    Rob. In the swan's -down, and tomb thee in arms.
    Countess. Then folks shall pray In vain to send me rest.
Away! your'e such another meddling lord.
    Rob. By heav'n, my love's as chaste as thou art lair,
And both exceed comparison! By this kiss,
That crowns me monarch of another world,
Superior to the first, fair, thou shalt see,
As unto heav'n my love, so unto thee.

----

   [8] The quartos read *his*; and the line, standing thus, might refer to Hercules and the Hesperian Fruit, were Hercules one of "feminine deities." The allusion, however, is evidently to Venus.

   [9] It is a vulgar belief, that a man is destined to have as many wives, as there appear wrinkles in his forehead when he frowns.

Countess. Alas, poor creatures! when we are once o' the falling hand,
A man may easily come over us;
It is as hard for us to hide our love,
As to shut sin from the Creator's eyes.
I'faith, my lord, I had a month's mind unto you,
As tedious as a full-rip'd maidenhead;
And, Count of Cyprus, think my love as pure
As the first opening of the blooms in May,
Your virtues' May;—nay, let me not blush to say so.
And see, for your sake, thus I leave to sorrow;—
Begin this subtle conjuration with me;
And as this taper, due unto the dead,
I here extinguish, so my late dead lord
I put out ever from my memory,
That his remembrance may not wrong our loves;

[Puts out one of the Tapers.

As bold-fac'd women, when they wed another,
Banquet their husbands with their dead loves' heads.
 Rob. And, as I sacrifice this to his ghost,
With this expire all corrupt thoughts of youth,
That fame-insatiate devil, Jealousy,
And all the sparks that may bring unto flame
Hate betwixt man and wife, or breed defame.

[Puts out the other Taper.[10]

Re-enter ROGERO and GUIDO.

 Guido. Marry, amen, I say! Madam, are you, that were in for all day, now come to be in for all night? How now, Count Arsena?
 Rog. Faith, signor, not unlike the condenin'd malefactor,
That hears his judgment openly pronounc'd;
But, I ascribe't to fate.—Joy swell your love,
Cyprus; and willow grace my drooping crest.
 Rob. We do intend our Hymeneal rites

---

[10] This Stage-direction does not occur in the original, but the text evidently requires it.

With the next rising sun.—Count Arsena,
Next to our bride, the welcom'st to our feast.

[Exeunt Roberto and Isabella.

Rog. Sancta Maria, what think'st thou of this change?
A player's passion I'll believe hereafter,
And in a tragic scene weep for old Priam,
When fell, revenging Pyrrhus, with suppos'd
And artificial wounds, mangles his breast;[11]
And think it a more worthy act in me,
Than trust a female mourning o'er her love.
Nought that is done of woman shall me please;
Nature's step-children rather her desire.

Guido. Learn of a well-composed epigram,
A woman's love; and thus 'twas sung unto us:—

> *The tapers that stood on her husband's hearse*
>   *Is' bell advances to a second bed;*
> *It is not wond'rous strange for to rehearse*
>   *She should so soon forget her husband, dead*
> *One hour. For if the husband's life once fade,*
> *Both love and husband in one grave are laid.*

But we forget ourselves; I'm for the marriage.
Of Signor Claridiana and the fine Mrs. Abigail.

Rog. I for his arch-foe's wedding, Signor Mizaldus, and the spruce Mrs. Thais. But see, the solemn rites are ended, and from their several temples they are come.

Guido. A quarrel, on my life.

Enter, at one door, SIGNOR CLARIDIANA, ABIGAIL, *his wife, and the* LADY LENTULUS, *with Rosemary,*[12] *as from Church;—at the other door,*

---

[11] The *Player's* speech in "Hamlet" seems here to bare been in Marston's thoughts; or, perhaps, a scene in Marlowe's "Dido," wherein a description of Priam's death is given by Œneas.

[12] Rosemary was formerly worn both at funerals and weddings, because, being said to strengthen the memory, when used medicinally, it was looked upon as an emblem of fidelity and remembrance.

17

SIGNOR MIZALDUS, THAIS, *his wife, and* MENDOSA FOSCARII, *from the bridal.—They see one another, and draw;* ROGERO *and the others step between them.*[13]

Cla. Good my lord, detain me not; I will tilt at him.

Rog. Remember, sir, this is your wedding-day, And that triumph belongs only to your wife.

Miz. If you be noble, let me cut off his head.

Guido. Remember, o'the other side, you have a maidenhead of your own to cut off.

Miz. I'll make my marriage-day like to the bloody bridal,
Alcides by the fiery Centaurs had.

Thais. Husband, dear husband!

Miz. Away with these caterwaulers! Come on, sir!

Cla. Thou son of a Jew,—

Guido. Alas, poor wench, thy husband's circumcis'd!

Cla. Begot when thy father's face was tow'rd the East,
To shew that thou would'st prove a caterpillar;[14]
His Messias shall not save thee from me,
I'll send thee to him in collops!

Rog. Oh, fry not in choler so, sir!

Miz. Mountebank, with thy pedantical action! *Rimatrix, Buglors, Rhimocers!*

Men. Gentlemen, I conjure you, by the virtues of men!

Miz. Shall any broken quacksalver's[15] bastard oppose him to me in my nuptials? No! but I'll shew him better metal than ere the gallimaufrey his father used. Thou scum of his melting-pots, that wert christened in a crusoile with Mercury-water, to shew thou would'st prove a stinging aspis,—for all thou spitt'st is aqua-fortis, and thy breath is a compound of poisons stillatory,—if I get within thee, had'st thou the scaly hide of a crocodile, as

---

[13] This is an instance of the confusion with regard to the scene of action, which exists in most of our old plays. *Rogero* and *Guido* have not stirred from the *Countess's* chamber, and yet we here see the bridal arties entering, as if in the open street. An inscription displayed on a board, probably, was deemed sufficient notification to the audience of the change of scene.

[14] "Caterpillar—an envious person, that does mischief without provocation."—BAILEY.

[15] A mountebank or quack.

thou art partly of his nature, I would leave thee as bare as an anatomy at the second viewing.

Cla. Thou Jew of the tribe of Gad, that, I am sure, were there none here but thou and I, would'st teach me the art of breathing; thou would'st run like a dromedary.

Miz. Thou, that art the tallest[16] man of Christendom, when thou art alone, if thou dost maintain this to my face, I'll make thee skip like an Ounce.

Men. Nay, good sir, be you still!

Miz. Let the quacksalver's son he still; his father was 'still, and 'still, and 'still again.

Cla. By the Almighty, I'll study necromancy, be reveng'd!

Rog. Gentlemen, leave these dissensions! Signor Mizaldus, you're a man of note.

Cla. True, all the city points at him for a knave.

Rog. You are of like reputation, Signor Claridiana;
The hatred, 'twixt your grandsires first began,
Impute it to the folly of that age;
These your dissensions may erect a faction,
Like to the Capulets and Montagues.

Men. Put it to arbitration, choose your friends;
The Senators will think' em happy in't.

Miz. I'll ne'er embrace the smoke of a furnace, the quintessence of minerals or simples, or, as I may say more learnedly, the spirit of quicksilver.

Cla. Nor I, such a centaur, half a man, half an ass, and all a Jew.

Rog. Nay, then we will be constables, and force a quiet. Gentlemen, keep 'em asunder, and help to persuade 'em!

(Rogero *forces* Claridiana *off at one door; and* Guido, Mizaldus, *at the other.*)

Men. Well, ladies, your husbands behave 'em as lustily on their wedding-days, as e'er I heard any.—Nay, lady widow, you and I must have a falling; you're of Signor Claridiana's faction, and I am your vowed enemy, from the bodkin to the pincase. Hark, in your ear!

[Mendosa *and* Lady Lentulus *talk apart.*

---

16 *i. e.* the boldest.

Abig. Well, Thais! Oh, you are a cunning carver! We two, that, any time, these fourteen years, have been called sisters, brought and bred up together; that have told one another all our wanton dreams; talk'd all night long of young men; and spent many an idle hour fasted upon the stones on St. Agnes' night together;[17] practiced all the petulant amorousnesses that delight young maids; yet have you concealed, not only the marriage, but the man; and well you might deceive me, for I'll be sworn you never dreamed of him: and it stands against all reason you should enjoy him you never dreamed of.

Thais. Is not all this the same in you? Did you ever manifest your sweetheart's nose, that I might nose him by't? commend his calf, or his nether lip? apparent signs that, you were not in love, or wisely covered it. Have you ever said, such a man goes upright, or has a better gait than any of the rest? as indeed since he is proved a Magnifico: I thought thou would'st have put it into my hands, whate'er't had been.

Abig. Well, wench, we have cross fates, our husbands such inveterate foes, and we such entire friends; but, the best is, we are neighbours, and our back-arbours may afford visitation freely.[18] Pr'ythee, let us maintain our familiarity still, whatsoever thy husband do unto thee, as I am afraid he will cross it i'the nick.

Thais. Faith, you little one, if I please him in one thing, he shall please me in all, that's certain! Who shall I have to keep my counsel, if I miss thee? Who should teach me to use the bridle, when the reins are in my own hand? What to long for? When to take physic? Where to be melancholy? Why, we two are one another's grounds,[19] without which, would be no music.

---

[17] They who wish for an explanation of this passage, I may consult any of the popular tracts relative to the superstitious ceremonies performed by girls, who are anxious to ascertain the names of their destined husbands.

[18] Our old dramatists, continually introduce in foreign countries the customs, &c. of their own. These back-arbours were doubtless better known to the ladies of London, than to those of Venice. Nash, in his "Anatomie of Abuses," 1595, speaking of the citizens' wives, says, "In the fields and suburbs, they have gardens, either paled or walled round about very high, with their harbers and bowers fit arise purpose."

[19] "GROUND—The plain-song; the tune on which descants are raised." JOHNSON— "On that *ground* I'll make a holy descant."—*Richard III. Act.* 3.

Abig. Well said, wench! and the prick-songs[20] we use shall be our husbands'.

Thais. I will long for swine's-flesh, o'the first child.

Abig. Wilt thou, little Jew? And I, to kiss thy husband, upon the least belly-ache. This will mad 'em.

Thais. I kiss thee, wench, for that, and with it confirm our friendship.

*(They talk apart.—*Mendosa *and* Lady Lentulus *come forward.)*

Men. By these sweet lips, widow!

Lady Len. O, good my lord, you learn to swear by rote.
Your birth and fortune make my brain suppose
That, like a man heated with wines and lust,
She that is next your object, is your mate,
Till the foul water have quenched out the fire.
You, the Duke's kinsman, tell me I am young,
Fair, rich, and virtuous; I myself will flatter
Myself, till you are gone, that are more fair,
More rich, more virtuous, and more debonair;
All which are ladders to a higher reach.
Who drinks a puddle, that may taste a spring?
Who kiss a subject, that may hug a king?

Men. Yes, the camel always drinks in puddle-water;
And as for huggings, read antiquities.
"Faith! madam, I'll board thee one of these days.

Lady Len. Ay, but, ne'er bed me, my lord; my vow is firm,
Since God hath call'd me to this noble state,
Much to my grief, of virtuous widowhood,
No man shall overcome within my gates.

Men. Wilt thou ram up thy porch-hold? O widow,
I perceive you're ignorant of the lover's legerdemain.
There is a fellow that by magic will assist to, murther princes invisible; I can
   command his spirit.
Or, what say you to a fine scaling ladder if ropes?

---

[20] Prick-song is a song pricked, or taken down in notes.

I can tell you I'm mad wag-halter.
But, by the virtue I see seated in you,
And by the worthy fame is blazon'd of you,
By little Cupid, that is mighty nam'd,
And can command my looser follies down,
I love, and must enjoy; yet, with such limits,
As one that knows enforced marriage
To be the Furies' sister. Think of me!

 Abig. and Thais. Ha! ha! ha!

 Men. How now, ladies, does the toy take you, as they say?

 Abig. No, my lord; nor do we take your toy, as they say. This is a child's birth, that must not be delivered before a man; though your lordship might be a midwife, for your chin.

 Men. Some bawdy riddle, is't not? You long till it be night.

 Thais. No, my lord, women's longing comes after their marriage night. —— (*To Abig.*) Sister, see you be constant now.

 Abig. Why, dost think I'll make my husband a cuckold? Oh! here they come.

  Re-enter, at one door, ROGERO *and* CLARIDIANA; *at the other,*
    GUIDO *and* MIZALDUS.

 Men. Signor Mizaldus, are you yet qualified?

 Miz. Yes! does any man think I'll go like a sheep to the slaughter? Hands off, my lord! your lordship may chance come under my hands: if you do, I shall shew myself a citizen, and revenge basely.

 Cla. I think, if I were receiving the holy Sacrament, his sight would make me gnash my teeth terribly.
But there's the beauty without parallel, (*Aside, gazing at Thais.*)
In whom the Graces and the Virtues meet;
In her aspéct mild Honour sits, and smiles;
And who looks there, were it the savage bear,
But would derive new nature from her eyes?
But, to be reconcil'd simply for her!
Were mankind to be lost again, I'd let it,
And a new heap of stones should stock the world.

In heav'n and earth this power beauty hath,
It inflames temperance, and temp'rates wrath.
Whate'er thou art, mine art thou, wise or chaste!
I shall set hard upon thy marriage-vow,
And write Revenge high in thy husband's brow,
In a strange character. —— *(To Men.)* You may begin, Sir.
   Men. Signor Claridiana, I hope Signor Mazildus
Has employ'd me about a good office;
'Twere worthy Cicero's tongue, a famous oration now;
But friendship, that is mutually embraced of the gods,
And is Jove's usher to each sacred synod,
Without the which he could not reign in heaven,
That overgoes my admiration, shall not undergo my censure.
Quench these hot flames of rage, that else will be
As fire amidst your nuptial jollity,
Burning the edge off from the present joy,
And keep you 'wake to terror.
   Cla. I have not yet swallowed the Rhimatrix, nor the Onocentaur; the
Rhinoceros was monstrous.
   Rog. Sir, be you of the more flexible nature, and confess an error.
   Cla. I must; the God of Love commands,
And that bright star, her eye, that guides my fate.—*(Aside.)*
Signor Mizaldus! joy then, Signor Mizaldus!
   Miz. Signor, Sir! Oh, devil!
   Thais. Good husband, shew yourself a temp'rate man!
Your mother was a woman, I dare swear;
No tyger got you, nor no bear was rival
In your conception; you seem like the issue
The painters limn leaping from Envy's mouth,
That devours all he meets.
   Miz. Had but the last or the least syllable
Of this more than immortal eloquence
Commenc'd to me, when rage had been so high
Within my blood, that it o'er—topt my soul,
Like to the lion, when he hears the sound

Of Dian's bowstring in some shady wood,
I should have couch'd my lowly limbs on earth,
And held my silence a proud sacrifice.

    Cla. Slave, I will fight with thee at any odds;
Or, name an instrument fit for destruction,
That ne'er was made to make away a man.
I'll meet thee on the ridges of the Alps,
Or some inhospitable wilderness,
Stark-nak'd, at push of pike, or curtle-axe,
At Turkish sickle, Babylonian saw,
The ancient hooks of great Cadwallader,
Or any other heathen invention.

    Thais. Oh, God bless the man!

    Lady Len. Counsel him, good my lord.

    Men. Our tongues are weary, and he desperate;
He does refuse to hear: what shall we do?

    Cla. I am not mad! I can hear, I can see, I can eel.
But a wise rage in man, wrongs past compare,
Should be well nourished, as his virtues are.
I'd have it known unto each valiant spright,
He wrongs no man that to himself does right.
Catzo![21] I ha' done, Signor Mizaldus, I ha' done.

    Rog. By heav'n, this voluntary reconciliation, made
Freely and of itself, argues unfeign'd
And virtuous knot of love; so, sirs, embrace.

    Cla. Sir, by the conscience of a Catholic man,
And by our mother Church, that binds,
And doth atone in amity with God
The souls of men, that they with men be one,
I tread into the centre all the thoughts
Of ill in me tow'rd you, and memory
Of what from you might aught disparage me;
Wishing, unfeignedly, it may sink low,

---

[21] *Catzo*—Ital. Cazzo—Membrum virile. The word is commonly thus used, as an expression of defiance and contempt, by the lower orders of the Italians.

And, as untimely births, want power to grow.

Men. Christianly said. Signor, what would you have more?

Miz. And so, I swear, you're honest, Onocentaur.

Rog. Nay, see now, fie upon your turbulent spirit! Did he do't in this form?

Miz. If you think not this sufficient, you shall command me to be reconciled in another form, as a Rhimatrix, or a Rhinoceros.

Men. 'Sblood, what will you do?

Cla. Well, give me your hand first; I am friends with you, i'faith; thereupon; I embrace you; kiss your wife; and God give us joy. *(To Thais.)*

Thais. You mean me and my husband.

Cla. You take the meaning better than the speech, lady.

Miz. The like wish I, but ne'er can be the like; and therefore wish I thee ——

Cla. By this bright light that is deriv'd from thee,—

Thais. So, sir, you make me a very light creature.

Cla: But that thou art a blessed angel, sent
Down from the gods, t'atone for mortal men,
I would have thought deeds beyond all men's thoughts,
And executed more upon his corps.
Oh, let him thank the beauty of this eye;
And not his resolute; sword or destiny.

Rog. What say'st thou, Guido? Come, applaud this jubilee; a day, these hundred years before not truly known to these divided factions.

Cla. (Aside.) No! nor this day, had it been falsely borne,
But that I mean to sound it with his horn.

Guido. I lik'd the former jar better; then they shewed like men and soldiers, now like cowards and lechers.

Rog. Well said, Guido! thou art like the bass viol in a concert; let the other instruments ravish and delight in the highest sense, thou art still grumbling.

Miz. (Aside to Abig. Offering her a Letter.) Nay, sweet, receive it, and in't my heart;
And when thou read'st a moving syllable,
Think that my soul was secretary to't.
It is your love, and not the odious wish
Of my revenge, in stiling him a cuckold,
Makes me presume thus far; then read it, fair!

My passion's ample as your beauties are.

    Abig. (*Aside to Miz.*) Well, Sir, I will not stick with you.

    Rog. And, gentlemen, since it hath happ'd so fortunately,

I do entreat we may all meet tomorrow,

In some heroic Masque, to grace the nuptials

Of the most noble Count of Cyprus.[22]

    Men. Who does the young Count marry?

    Rog. Who but the very heir of all her sex,

That bears the palm of beauty from them fall?

Others, compar'd to her, shew like faint stars,

To the full moon of wonder in her face.

The Lady Isabella, the late widow

To the deceas'd and noble Viscount Hermus.

    Men. La' you there, widow, there's one of the last edition,

Whose husband yet retains in his cold trunk

Some little airing of his noble guest,

Yet she a fresh bride as the month of May.

    Lady Len. Well, my lord, I am none of these,

That have my second husband yet bespoke;

My door shall be a testimony of it;

And, but these noble marriages incite me,

My much-abstracted presence should have shew'd it.

If you come to me, heark in your ear, my lord,

Look your ladder of ropes be strong,

For I shall tie you to your tackling. [*Aside to Men.*

    Rog. Gentlemen, your answer to the Masque.

    Omnes. Your honour leads, we'll follow.

    Miz. Signor Claridiana.

    Cla. I attend you, sir.

    Thais. (*To Cla.*) You'll be constant.

[Exeunt all but Cla.

    Cla. Above the ad'mant; goat's-blood shall not break me.

Yet, shallow fools, and plainer moral men,

---

[22] The 4to. 1631 reads—

"Of the most noble Countess of Suevia."

That understand not what they undertake,
Fall in their own snares, or come short of vengeance.
No! let the sun view with an open face,
And afterwards shrink in his blushing cheeks,
Asham'd, and cursing of the fix'd decree,
That makes his light bawd to the crimes of men.
When I have ended what I now devise,
Apollo's oracle shall swear me wise.
Strumpet his wife, branch my false-seeming friend,
And make him foster what my hate begot,—
A bastard, that, when age and sickness seize him,
Shall be a corr'sive to his griping heart.
I'll write to her; for, what her modesty
Will not permit, nor my adult'rate forcing,
That blushless herald shall not fear to tell.
Mizaldus shall know yet, his foe's a man,
    And, what is more, a true Italian.   [*Exit.*

END OF ACT I.

ACT II.

SCENE 1.—*Venice—An Apartment in the House of* Roberto.

Enter ROBERTO, *the* COUNTESS, *the* LORD CARDINAL, LADY LENTULUS, ABIGAIL, *and* THAIS.

Rob. My grave Lord Cardinal, we congratulate,
And zealously do entertain your love,
That, from your high and divine contemplation,
You have vouchsaf'd to consummate a day,
Due to our nuptials. Oh! may this knot you knit,
This individual, Gordian grasp of hands,
In sight of God so fairly intermix'd,
Never be sever'd (as heav'n smiles at it,)
By all the darts shot by infernal Jove!
Angels of grace, Amen, Amen, say to't!
Fair lady widow, and my worthy mistress,
Do you keep silence for a wager?

Thais. Do you ask a woman that question, my lord, when she inforcedly pursues what she's for bidden? I think, if I had been tied to silence, I should have been worthy the cucking-stool[23] ere this time.

Rob. You shall not be my orator, lady, that plead thus for yourself.

Enter a SERVANT.

Ser. My lord, the Masquers are at hand.
Rob. Give them kind entertainment.   [*Exit Ser.*
Some worthy friends of mine, my lord,
Unknown to me, too lavish of their loves,
Bring their own welcome in a solemn Masque.

---

[23] Cucking-stool is synonimous with ducking-stool, the well-known punishment of a scold.

Abig. I am glad there's noblemen i'the Masque with our husbands, to overrule them; they had sham'd us all else.

Thais. Why for why, I pray?

Abig. Why?—Marry, they had come in with some city shew else; hired a few tinsel coats at the, vizard-maker's, which would ha' made them look, for all the world, like bakers, in their linen bases[24] and mealy vizards, new come from boulting. I saw a show once at the marriage of a Magnifico's daughter, presented by Time, which Time was an old bald thing: a servant 'twas: The best man was a dyer, and came, in likeness of the rainbow, in all manner of colours, to shew his art; but the rainbow smelled of urine; so we were all afraid the property was changed, and looked for a shower. Then came in after him, one that, it seemed, feared no colours; a grocer; that had trimm'd up himself handsomely; he was Justice, and shew'd reasons why. And I think this grocer—I mean this Justice—had borrow'd a weather-beaten balance from some Justice of a conduit, both which scales were replenish'd with the choice of his ware; and, the more liberally to shew his nature, he gave every woman in the room her handful.

Thais. Oh, great act of justice! Well, an my husband come cleanly off with this, he shall ne'er betray his weakness more, but confess himself a citizen hereafter, and acknowledge their lack of wit; for, alas! they come short.

Enter, in the Masque, ROGERO, MENDOSA, MIZALDUS *and* CLARI-DIANA *as Torch-bearers; they deliver their Shields to their several Mistresses; that is to say—*ROGERO *to the* COUNTESS, MENDOSA *to* LADY LENTULUS, CLARIDIANA *to* THAIS, *and* MIZALDUS *to* ABIGAIL.

Countess. Good my lord, be my expositor.

[To the Cardinal.

Cardinal. The sun setting, a man pointing at it;
The Motto—*Senso tamen ipse calorem.*
Fair bride, some servant of yours, that here intimates
To have felt the heat of love, bred by your brightness;

---

[24] Gifford, in a Note on Jonson's "Poetaster," says that bases were a kind of short petticoats, somewhat like the phillibegs of the Highlanders. I am, however, inclined to think, from this and other passages in which the word occurs, that *bases* were loose trowsers

But, setting thus from him by marriage,
He only here acknowledgeth your power,
And must expect beams of a morrow sun.

Lady Len. Lord bridegroom, will you interpret me.

Rob. A sable shield; the word—*Vidua spes.*
What! the forlorn hope, in black, despairing?
Lady Lentulus, is this the badge of all your suitors?

Lady Len. Ay, by my troth, my lord, if they come to me.

Rob. I could give it another interpretation. Methinks, this lover has learned of women to deal by contraries if so, then here he says; the Widow is his only hope.

Lady Len. No, good my lord, let the first stand.

Rob. Inquire of him, and he'll resolve the doubt.

Abig. What's here? a ship sailing nigh her haven? With good ware, belike; 'tis well ballast.

Thais. Oh! this your device smells of the merchant. What's your ship's name, I pray? the, Forlorn Hope?

Abig. No, the Merchant Royal.

Thais. And why not Adventurer?

Abig. You see there's no likelihood of that; would it not fain be in the haven? The word—*Ut tangerem portum!* Marry, for aught I know, God grant it! What's there?

Thais. Mine's an azure shield. Marry, what else? I should tell thee more than I understand; but the word is, *Aut pretio, aut precibus.*

Abig. Ay, ay, some Common-Council device.

(They take the Women, and dance the First Change.)

Men. Fair widow, how like you this change?

Lady Len. I chang'd too lately, to like any.

Men. Oh, your husband! you wear his memory like a Death's-head.
For heav'n's love, think of me, as of the man
Whose dancing days you see are not yet done.

Lady Len. Yet you sink apace,[25] sir.

---

[25] The Widow is punning upon the name of a Dance called the *Sinque-apace.*

Men. The fault's in my upholsterer, lady.

Cla. (To Thais.) Thou shalt as soon find Truth telling a lie;
Virtue, a bawd; Honesty, a courtier;
As me turu'd recreant to thy least design:
Love makes me speak; and he makes Jove divine.

Thais. Would, love could make you so; but 'tis his guise,
To let us surfeit, ere he ope our eyes.

[They talk apart.

Abig. (To Miz.) You grasp my hand too hard, i'faith, fair sir.

Miz. Not as you grasp my heart, unwilling wanton.
Were but my breast bare, and anatomiz'd,
Thou should'st behold there how thou tortur'st it;
And, as Apelles limn'd the Queen of Love
In her right hand grasping a heart in flames,
So may I thee, fairer but crueller!

Abig. Well sir, your vizard gives you colour for what you say.

Miz. Grace me to wear this favour! 'tis a gem
That vails[26] to your eyes, though not to th'eagle's;
And, in exchange, give me one word of comfort.

Abig. Ay, marry, I like this wooer well; he'll win his pleasure out o'the stones.

(The Second Change.—The Countess *falls in love with* Rogero *when the Changers speak.)*

Countess. (Aside.) Change is no robbery; yet, in this Change
Thou robb'st me of my heart! Sure, Cupid's here,
Disguised like a pretty torch-bearer;
And makes his brand a torch; that, with more sleight,
He may intrap weak women. Here the sparks
Fly, as in Ætna from his father's anvil.
O pow'rful boy, my heart's on fire; and unto mine eyes
The raging flames ascend, like to two beacons,
Summoning my strongest pow'rs, but all too late;

---

[26] "VAIL"– To put off the hat; to strike sail; *to give sign of submission.*"—Bullokar's English Expositor, 1616.

31

The conquerer already opes the gate.
I will not ask his name.

Abig. (to Miz.) You dare put it in my hands!

Miz. Zounds! do you think I will not?

Abig. Then thus to-morrow,—you'll be secret, servant!

Miz. All that I do, I'll do in secret.

Abig.—My husband goes to Maurano, to renew the farm he has.

Miz. Well, what time goes the jakes'-farmer?

Abig. He shall not be long out, but you shall put in, I warrant you; have a care that you stand just i' the nick. About six o'clock in the evening, my maid shall conduct you up. To save mine honour, you must come up darkling, and to avoid suspicion.

Miz. Zounds, hoodwink'd, an you'll open, all, sweet lady!

Abig. But, if you fail to do't.

Miz. The sun shall fail the day first.

Abig. Tie this ring fast, you may be sure to know.
You'll brag of this, now you have brought me to the bay.

[They talk apart.

Cla. Pox o'this Masque! Would 'twere done, that I might to my apothecary's for some stirring meats!

Thais. Methinks, sir, you should blush, e'en through your vizor. I have scarce patience to dance out the rest.

Cla. The worse my fate, that plough a marble quarry:
Pygmalion, yet thy image was more kind,
Although thy love not half so true as mine!
Dance they that list; I sail against the wind.

Thais. Nay, sir, betray not your infirmities!
You'll make my husband jealous by and by.
We'll think of you, and that presently.

Rog. The spheres ne'er danc'd unto a better tune. Sound music there!

(The Third Change ended, the Ladies fall off.)

Countess. (Aside.) 'Twas music that he spake.

Rob. Gallants, I thank you, and begin, a health to your mistresses!

Three or Four. Fair thanks, sir bridegroom!

32

Countess. (Aside.) He speaks not to this pledge! has he no mistress?
Would I might choose one for him! but it may be,
He doth adore a brighter star than me.

Rob. Sit, ladies, sit! you have had standing long.

*(*Rogero *dances a Levalto*[27] *or a Galliard, and in the midst of it falleth into
the bride's lap; but straight leaps up, and danceth it out.)*

Men. Bless the man; spiritedly and nobly done!

Thais. What, is your ladyship hurt?

Countess. Oh, no! an easy fall.—
Was I not deep enough, thou god of lust,
But I must farther wade? I am his now,
As sure as Juno's Jove's! Hymen, take flight,
And see not me! 'tis net my wedding night.

[Aside, and Exit.

Card. The bride's departed discontent, it seems.

Rob. We'll after her. Gallants, unmask, I pray;
And taste a homely banquet, we entreat.

[Exit Rob *and the* Cardinal.

Cla. Candied eringoes, I beseech thee!

Men. Come, widow, I'll be hold to put you in.
My lord, will you have a sociate.   *[To* Rog.

[Exit Men. *with* Lady Len. A big. *and* Thais.

Rog. Good gentlemen, if I have any interest in you,
Let me depart unknown! 'Tis a disgrace
Of an eternal memory.

Miz. What, the fall, my lord? As common a thing as can be! The stiffest
man in Italy may fall between a woman's legs.

Cla. Would I had changed places with you, my lord! Would it had been
my hap!

---

[27] Sir J. Davies, in his "Orchestra" gives a very particular description of the *Levalto* or
Lavolta, from which it would appear to have exactly resembled the modern *Waltz*. The text,
however, proves that a *pas seul* was sometimes so termed. A *Galliard* (which is also described
by Sir J. D.) was a sprightly dance, with much turning and capering.

Rog. What cuckold laid his horns in my way? Signor Claridiana, you were
by the lady when I fell; do you think I hurt her?

Cla. You could not hurt her, my lord, between the legs.

Rog. What was't I fell withal!

Miz. A cross point, my lord.

Rog. Cross point, indeed!
Well, if you love me, let me hence, unknown;
The silence your's, and the disgrace mine own!

[Exeunt Cla. and Miz.

Enter the COUNTESS *with a gilt Goblet, and meets* ROGERO.

Countess. If wine were nectar, I'd begin a health
To her that were most gracious in your eye;
Yet, deign, as simply 'tis the gift of Bacchus,
To give her pledge that drinks. This god of wine
Cannot inflame me more to appetite
(Though he be co-supreme with mighty love)
Than thy fair shape.

Rog. Zounds; she comes to deride me!

Countess. This kiss shall serve
To be a pledge, although my lips should starve.
No trick to get that vizard from his face?

Roy. I will steal hence, and so conceal disgrace.

Countess. Sir, have you left nought behind?

Rog. Yes, but the Fates will not permit
(As gems once lost are seldom or ne'er found)
I should convey it with me. Sweet, good night!
She bends to me: there's my fall again!

[Exit.

Countess. He's gone! like lightning, that awhile doth strike
Our amaz'd eyes with brightness; and on a sudden
Leaves us in prison'd darkness. Lust, thou art high!
My similes may well come from the sky.—
Anna! Anna!

34

Enter ANNA.

Anna. Madam, did you call?

Countess. Follow yon stranger! Pr'ythee, learn his name!
We may hereafter thank him. (*Exit* Anna.) How I doat!
Is he not a god,
That can command what other men would win
With the hard'st advantage? I must have him,
Or, shadow-like, follow his fleeting steps.
Were I as Daphne, and he follow'd chase,
(Though I rejected young Apollo's love,
And like a dream beguil'd his wand'ring steps,)
Should he pursue me though the neighb'ring grove,
Each cowslip-stalk should trip a willing fall,
Till he were mine, who till then am his thrall.
Nor will I blush, since worthy is my choice.
'Tis said that Venus with a Satyr slept;
And how much short came she of my fair aim!
Then, Queen of Love, a precedent I'll be,
To teach fair women learn to love of me!

Re-enter ANNA.

Speak, music, what's his name?

Anna. Madam, it was the worthy Count Arsena.

Countess. Bless'd be thy tongue! the worthy Count indeed!
The worthiest of the worthies! Trusty Anna,
Hast thou pack'd up those monies, plate, and jewels,
I gave direction for?

Anna. Yes, madam, I have truss'd up them, that many a proper man has been truss'd up for.

Countess. I thank thee!—Take the wings of night,
Beloved secretary, and post with them to Pavia;
There furnish up some stately palace,
Worthy to entertain the King of Love;
Prepare it for my coming and my love's.

35

Ere Phebus' steeds once more unharness'd be,
Or ere he sport with his beloved Thetis,
The silver-footed goddess of the sea,
We will set forward. Fly like the northern wind!
Or swifter, Anna, fleet like to my mind!

    Anna. I am just of your mind, madam: I am gone!   [*Exit.*

    Countess. So to the house of death the mourner goes,
That is bereft of what his soul desir'd,
As I to bed; ay, to my nuptial bed,
The heav'n on earth. So to thought-slaughter went
The pale Andromeda, bedew'd with tears,
When every minute she expected gripes
Of a fell monster; and in vain bewail'd
The act of her creation. Sullen night,
That look'st with sunk eyes on my nuptial bed,
With ne'er a star that smiles upon the end,
Mend thy slack pace! and lend the malcontent,
The hoping lover, and the wishing bride,
Beams, that too long thou shadowest! Or, if not,
In spite of thy fix'd front, when my loath'd mate
Shall, struggle in due pleasure for his right,
I'll think't my love, and die in that delight.

                                        [*Exit.*

SCENE 2.—*Venice.—An Apartment in the House of* Mizaldus.

Enter, at opposite Doors, ABIGAIL *and* THAIS.

    Abig. Thais, you're an early riser; I have that to shew, will make your hair stand on end.

    Thais. Well, lady, and I have that to shew you, will bring your courage down. What would you say, an I could name a party, saw your husband court, kiss, nay, almost go through for the hole?

    Abig. How! how! What would I say? Nay, by this light, what would I not do? If ever amazon fought better, or more at the face, than I'll do, let me never be thought a new-married wife! Come, unmask her; 'tis some admirable creature, whose beauty you need not paint; I warrant you, 'tis done to your hand.

Thais. Would any woman but I be abus'd to her face? *(Aside.)*—Pr'ythee read the contents: know'st thou the character?

[*Gives her the letter.*

Abig. 'Tis my husband's hand, and a love-letter; but, for the contents, I find none in it. Has the lustful monster all back and belly-starv'd me thus? What defect does he see in me? I'll be sworn, wench, I am of as pliant and yielding a body to him, e'en which way he will; he may turn me as he list himself. What! and dedicate to thee? Ay, marry, here's a style so high, as a man cannot help a dog o'er it. He was wont to write to me in the city phrase—"My good Abigail." Here's "Astonishment of nature"— "Unparallel'd excellency"—and "Most unequall'd rarity of creation."— Three such words will turn any honest woman in the world a whore; for, a woman is never won, till she know not what to answer; and beshrew me, if I understand any of these. You are the party, I perceive; and here's a white sheet that your husband has promis'd me to do penance in; you must not think to dance the Shaking of the Sheets alone. Though there be not such rare phrases in it, 'tis more to the matter. A legible hand, but for the dash, or the short bawdy parentheses, as ever you saw; and to the purpose. He has not left out a prick, I warrant you, wherein he has promised to do me any good: but, the law's in mine own hand.

Thais. I ever thought, by his red heard, he would prove a Judas.[28] Here am I bought and sold! He makes much of me indeed! Well, wench, we were best wisely in time seek for prevention. I should be loath to take drink, and die on't, as I am afraid I shall, that he will lie with thee.

Abig. To be short, sweetheart, I'll be true to thee, though a liar to thy husband. I have signed your husband's bill, like a woodcock as he is; persuaded him (since nought but my love can assuage his violent passions) he should enjoy, like a private friend the pleasure of my bed. I told him, my husband was gone to Maurano to-day, to renew a farm he has; and, in the mean time, he

---

[28] The traitor Judas was always represented in old paintings, and on tapestry, as having a red beard, and red hair.

might be tenant at will, to use mine. This false fire has so took with him, that he's ravish'd afore he come. I have had stones on him, all red: dost know this?

[Shows the Ring.

Thais. Ay, too well; it blushes for its master.[29]

Abig. Now, my husband will be hawking about thee anon, and thou canst meet him closely.

Thais. By my faith, I would be loath, in the dark, an he knew me!

Abig. I mean thus:—the same occasion will serve him too: they are birds of a feather, and will fly together, I warrant thee, wench. Appoint him to come; say that thy husband's gone for Maurano: and tell me anon, if thou mad'st not his heart-blood spring, for joy, in his face.

Thais. I conceive you not, all this while.

Abig. Then, thou'rt a barren woman, and no marvel if thy husband love thee not. The hour for both to come, is six; a dark time, fit for purblind lovers; and with cleanly conveyance by the nigglers our maids, they shall be translated into our bed-chambers: your husband into mine, and mine into your's.

Thais. But, you mean they shall come in at the back-doors.

Abig. Who? our husbands? nay, an they come not in at the fore-doors, there will be no pleasure in't. But, we two will climb over our garden-pales, and come in that way; (the chastest that are in Venice will stray, for a good turn;) and thus wittily will we be bestowed: you into my house, to your husband; and I into your house, to my husband; and, I warrant thee, before a month come to an end, they'll crack louder of this night's lodging than the bedsteads.

Thais. All is if our maids keep secret.

Abig. Mine is a maid, I'll be sworn; she has kept her secrets hitherto.

Thais. Troth, and I never had any sea-captain boarded in my house.

Abig. Go to, then; and, the better to avoid suspicion, thus we must insist: they must, come up darkling, recreate themselves with their delight an hour or two, and after a million of kisses, or so ——

Thais. But, is my husband content to come darkling?

---

[29] The edition of 1613 has here a stage-direction—*Points to the ring*—which in that of 1631 is printed as part of the text.

38

Abig. What! not to save mine honour? He that will run through fire, as he has professed, will, by the heat of his love, grope in the dark. I warrant him, he shall save mine honour.

Thais. I am afraid my voice will discover me.

Abig. Why, then, you had best say nothing, and take it quietly when your husband comes.

Thais. Ay! but, you know, a woman cannot choose but speak, in these cases.

Abig. Bite in your nether lip, and I warrant you! Or make as if you were whiffling tobacco; or puich like me.—Gadso, I hear thy husband!

Thais. Farewell, wise woman!   [*Exit*.

Enter MIZALDUS.

Miz. Now 'gins my vengeance mount high in my lust.
'Tis a rare creature, she'll do't i'faith;
And I am arm'd at all points. A rare whiblin,[30]
To be reveng'd, and yet gain pleasure in't:
One height above revenge! Yet, what a slave am I!
Are there not younger brothers enough, but we must
Branch one another? Oh! but mine's revenge;
And, who on that does dream,
Must be a tyrant ever in extreme.—
Oh, my wife Thais! Get my breakfast ready; I must into the country, to a farm
I Have, some two miles off; and, as I think, shall not come home to-night.
Jacques, Jacques, get my vessel ready to row me down the river! Pr'ythee, make
haste, sweet girl.   [*Exit*.

Thais. So, there's one fool shipp'd away! Are your cross-points discovered? Get your breakfast ready! By this light, I'll tie you to hard fare! I have been too sparing of that you prodigally offer voluntarily to another. Well, you shall be a tame fool hereafter.
The finest sleight is when we first defraud:
Husband, to-night 'tis I must lie abroad.   [*Exit*.

---

[30] I never met with this strange word before, have little doubt that it is a typographical blunder, but I am not prepared to offer any plausible substitute.

SCENE 3.—*Venice.*—Roberto's *House.*

Enter the COUNTESS, *with a Letter, followed by a* PAGE.

Countess. Here, take this letter, bear it to the Count;
But, boy, first tell me, think'st thou I'm in love?
    Page. Madam, I cannot tell.
    Countess. Canst thou not tell? Dost thou not see my face?
Is not the face the index of the mind?
And canst thou not distinguish love by that?
    Page. No, madam.
    Countess. Then, take this letter, and deliver it
Unto the worthy Count. No, fie upon him!
Come back again! Tell me, why should'st thou think
That same's a love-letter?
    Page. I do not think so, madam.
    Countess. I know thou dost; for, thou dost ever use
To hold the wrong opinion. Tell me true,
Dost thou not think that letter is of love?
    Page. If you would have me think so, madam—yes.
    Countess. What, dost thou think thy Lady is fond?
Give me the letter,—thyself shall see it.
Yet, I should tear it in the breaking ope,
And make him lay a wrongful charge on thee,
And thou brok'st it open by the way,
And saw what heinous things I charge him with:
But, 'tis all one, the letter's not of love;
Therefore, deliver it unto himself,
And tell him he's deceiv'd, I do not love him:
But, if he think so, bid him come to me,
And I'll confute him straight; I'll shew him reasons;
I'll shew him plainly why I cannot love him.
And, if he hap to read it in thy hearing,
Or chance to tell thee that the words were sweet,
Do not thou then disclose my rude intent,
Under those syren words; and how I mean

To use him when I have him at my will;
For then thou wilt destroy the plot that's laid,
And make him fear to yield, when I do wish
Only to have him yield; for, when I have him,
None but myself shall know how I will use him.
Begone! why stay'st thou? Yet, return again.
    Page. Ay, madam.
    Countess. Why dost thou come again? I bade thee go.
If I say go, never return again!   [*Exit* Page.
My blood, like to a troubled ocean,
Cuff'd with the winds, uncertain where to rest,
Butts at the utmost share of every limb.
My husband's not the man I would have had!
Oh, my new thoughts to this brave sprightly lord!
What's fierce as that hid fire that lovers feel?
Where was my mind before? That refin'd judgment,
That represents rare objects to our passions?
Or did my lust beguile me of my sense,
Making me feast upon such dang'rous cates,
For present want, that needs must breed a surfeit?
How was I shipwreck'd? Yet, Isabella, think
Thy husband is a noble gentleman,
Young, wise, and rich: think what fate follows thee,
And nought but lust doth blind thy worthy love.
I will desist. Oh! no, it may not be:
Even a head-strong courser bears away
His rider, vainly striving him to stay;
Or, as a sudden gale thrusts into sea
The haven-touching bark, now near the lee;
So wav'ring Cupid brings me back amain,[31]
And purple Love resumes his darts again:
Here, of themselves, thy shafts come, as if shot:
Better than I, thy quiver knows 'em not.

----

[31] The 4tos. read, "back *again.*"

Enter ROGERO and the PAGE.

Page. Madam, the Count.
Rog. So fell the Trojan wand'rer on the Greek,
And bore away his ravish'd prize to Troy.
For such a beauty, brighter than his Danae,
Jove should, methinks, now come himself again.
Lovely Isabella, I confess me mortal,
Not worthy to serve thee in thought, I swear;
Yet, shall not this same over-flow of favour
Diminish my vow'd duty to your beauty.
Countess. Your love, my lord, I blushing proclaim it,
Hath power to draw me through a wilderness.
Wer't arm'd with furies, as with furious beasts.
Boy, bid our train be ready,—we'll to horse.

[Exit Page.

My lord, I should say something, but I blush;
Courting is not befitting to our sex.
Rog. I'll teach you how to woo.
Say you have lov'd me long;
And tell me that a woman's feeble tongue
Was never tuned unto a wooing string;
Yet, for my sake, you will forget your sex,
And court my love with strain'd immodesty;
Then bid me make you happy with a kiss.
Countess. Though women do not woo, yet, for your sake,
I am content to leave that civil custom,
And pray you kiss me.
Rog. Now use some unexpected ambages,
To draw me farther into Vulcan's net.
Countess. You love not me so well as I love you.
Rog. Fair lady, but I do.
Countess. Then, shew your love.
Rog. Why, in this kiss I shew't, and my vow'd service.
This wooing shall suffice: 'tis easier far
To make the current of a silver brook

42

Convert his flowing backward to his spring,
Than turn a woman wooer. There's no cause
Can turn the settled course of Nature's laws.

    Countess. My lord, will you pursue the plot?

    Rog. The letter gives direction here for Pavie.
To horse! to horse! Thus on Eurydice,
With looks regardant, did the Thracian gaze,
And lost his gift, while he desired the sight.
But wiser, I, led by more powerful charms,
I'd see the world win thee from out mine arms.

[Exeunt.

SCENE 4.—*A Hall in* Roberto's *House.—A trampling of Horses heard.*

Enter, at opposite doors, CLARIDIANA *and* GUIDO.

    Guido. Zounds, is the hurricane coming? Claridiana, what's the matter.

    Cla. The Countess of Suevia has new taken horse.—
Fly Phœbus, fly, the hour is six o'clock.

    Guido. Whither is she gone, signori?[32]

    Cla. Even as Jove went to meet his Semele:—
To the devil, I think.

    Guido. You know not wherefore?

    Cla. To say sooth, I do not:—
So in immortal wise shall I arrive.

    Guido. At the gallows. What, in a passion, signer?

    Cla. Zounds, do not hold me, sir:—
Beauteous Thais, I am all thine wholly.
The staff is now advancing for the rest,
And when I tilt, Mizaldus, 'ware thy crest.[33]

[Exit.

    Guido. What's here? the cap'ring god-head[34] tilting in the air?

---

[32] The 4to. 1613, reads, "Whither is she *going.*"

[33] Claridiana here borrows his figures from the language of the tilt-yard.

[34] The 4to. 1613, reads, "cap'ring *cod's-head.*"

Enter ROBERTO, *in his night-gown and cap, with Servants: he kneels downs.*

 Rob. The gods send her remorse,[35] a poor old age,
Eternal woe, and sickness' lasting rage.
 Servant. My lord, you may yet o'er-take 'em.
 Rob. Furies supply that place, for I will not! No;
She that can forsake me when pleasure's in the full,
Fresh and untir'd, what would she on the least barren coldness?
I warrant you she has already got
Her bravoes, and her ruffians; the meanest whore
Will have one buckler, but your great ones more.
The shores of Sicily retain not such a monster,
Though to galley-slaves they daily prostitute.
To let the nuptial tapers give light to her new lust!
Who would have thought it? She that could no more
Forsake my company, than can the day
Forsake the glorious presence of the sun.
When I was absent, then her galled eyes
Would have shed April showers, and outwept
The clouds in that same over-passionate mood
When they drown'd all the world; yet, now forsakes me.
Women, your eyes shed glances like the sun;
Now shines your brightness, now your light is done;
On the sweet'st flow'rs you shine, 'tis but by chance;
And on the basest weed you'll waste a glance;
Your beams once lost, can never more be found,
Unless we wait until your course run round,
And take you at fifth hand. Since I cannot
Enjoy the noble title of a man;
But after-ages (as our virtues are
Buried whilst we are living) will sound out
My infamy, and her degen'rate shame;
Yet, in my life I'll smother't, if I may,

---

[35] The old copies read, "The gods send her *no horse*," which I have ventured to correct. The context I think will justify the alteration.

And like a dead man to the world bequeath
These houses of vanity, mills and lands.
Take what you will (I will not keep) among you, servants;
And welcome, some religious monastery.
A true-sworn beads-man I'll hereafter be,
And wake the morning cock with holy prayers.
 Servants. Good, my lord! noble master!
 Rob. Dissuade me not; my will shall be my king.
I thank thee, wife, a fair change thou hast given;
I leave thy lust, to woo the love of heaven.

[Exit, followed by the Servants.

 Guido. This is conversion, is't not? As good as might have been he turns religious upon his wife's turning courtezan. This is just like some of our gallant prodigals; when they have consumed their patrimonies wrongfully, they turn Capuchins for devotion. [Exit.

END OF ACT II.

ACT III.

SCENE 1.—*A Street in Venice.*—Claridiana *and* Mizaldus *being in readiness, are received in at one another's houses by their Maids.*

Then enter MENDOSA, *with a Page, to the* Lady Lentulus' *window.*

Men. Night, like a solemn mourner, frowns on earth,
Envying that day should force her doff her robes,
Or Phoebus chase away her melancholy.
Heaven's eyes look faintly through her sable mask,
And silver Cynthia hies her in her sphere,
Scorning to grace black night's solemnity.
Be unpropitious, night, to villain thoughts,
This is the lower house of high-built heaven,
Where my chaste Phœbe sits, enthron'd 'mong thoughts
So purely good, bring her to heaven on earth:
Such power in soul hath contemplation.
Sing, boy, (though't's night yet) like the morning's lark;
A soul that's clear is light, though heaven be dark.   [*Music plays.*

Enter LADY LENTULUS *above, at her window.*

Lady Len. Who speaks in music to us?
Men. Sweet, 'tis I. Boy, leave me, and to bed.   [*Exit Page.*
Lady Len. I thank you for your music: now, good night.
Men. Leave not the world yet, queen of chastity.
Keep promise with thy love Endymion,
And let me meet thee there on Latmus' top.
'Tis I, whose virtuous hopes are firmly fix'd
On the fruition of thy chaste-vow'd love.
Lady Len. Your honour made me promise your ascent
Into my house, since my vow barr'd my doors,
By some wit's engine, made for theft and lust;

Yet, for your honour, and my humble fame,
Check your bloods passions, and return, dear lord:
Suspicion is a dog that still doth bite
Without a cause; this act gives food to envy;
Swoll'n big, it bursts, and poisons our clear flames.
    Men. Envy is stingless, when she looks on thee.
    Lady Len. Envy is blind, my lord, and cannot see
    Men. If you break promise, fair, you break my heart.
    Lady Len. Then come. Yet stay. Ascend. Yet let us part.
I fear, my lord, yet know not what I fear:
Your love is precious, yet mine honour's dear.
    Men. If I do stain thy honour with foul lust,
May thunder strike me, to shew Jove is just!
    Lady Len. Then come, my lord, on earth your vow is given;
This aid I'll lend you.
    Men. Thus I mount my heaven.
Receive me, sweet!
        [*He throws up a ladder of cord, which she makes fast to some part of the*
                window: he ascends, and at the top falls.
    Lady Len. Oh! me, unhappy wretch.
How fares your honour? Speak, thou fate-cross'd lord!
If life retain his seat within you, speak!
Else, like that Sestian dame that saw her love
Cast by the frowning billows on the sands,
And lean death swollen big with the Hellesont,
In bleak Leander's body, like his love,
Come I to thee;—one grave shall serve us both.
    Men. Stay, miracle of women, yet I breath;
Though death be enter'd in this tower of flesh,
He is not conqueror; my heart stands out,
And yields to thee, scorning his tyranny.
    Lady Len. My doors are vow'd shut, and I cannot help you.
Your wounds are mortal; wounded is mine honour,
If there the town-guard find you. Hapless dame!
Relief is perjury,—my vow kept, shame.

47

What hellish destiny did twist my fate?

    Men. Rest seize thine eye-lids; be not passionate!
Sweet, sleep secure, I'll remove myself.
That viper, Envy, shall not spot thy fame:
I'll take that poison with me, my soul's rest,
For, like a serpent, I'll creep on my breast.

    Lady Len. Thou more than man! love-wounded, joy and grief
Fight in my blood. Thy wounds and constancy
Are both so strong, none can have victory.

    Men. Darken the world, earth's-queen! get thee to bed!
The earth is light, while those two stars are spread;
Their splendour will betray me to men's eyes.
Vail thy bright face; for, if thou longer stay,
Phœbus will rise to thee, and make night day.

    Lady Len. To part, and leave you hurt, my soul doth tear.

    Men. Depart from hence I cannot, you being there.

    Lady Len. We'll move together then; fate, love centrouls;
And, as we part, so bodies part from souls.

    Mine. Mine is the earth, thine the refined fire;
I'm mortal, thou divine; then, soul, mount higher!

    Lady Len. Why, then, take comfort, sweet; I'll see thee on to-morrow.

[Exit.

    Men. My wounds are nothing; thy loss breeds my sorrow.—
See, now 'tis dark!
Support your master, legs, a little farther!
Faint not, bold heart, with anguish of my wound!
Try farther yet! can blood weigh down my soul?
Desire is vain, without ability.
Thus falls a monarch, if fate push at him.

(He staggers on, and then falls down.)

Enter the Captain of the Watch, and his Men.

    Captain. Come on, my hearties! we are the city's security. I'll give you your
charge; and then, like courtiers, every man spy out. Let no man in my

company be afraid to speak to a cloak lined with velvet; nor tremble at the sound of a gingling spur.[36]

1st. Watch. May I never be counted a cock of the game, if I fear spurs; but be gelded like a capon, for the preserving of my voice.

Captain. I'll have none of my band refrain to search a venereal house, though his wife's sister he a lodger there; nor take two shillings of the bawd, to save the gentlemen's credits that are aloft: and so, like voluntary panders leave them, to the shame of all halbardiers.[37]

2nd Watch. Nay, for the wenches, we'll tickle them, that's flat.

Captain. If you meet a chevaliero, (that is, in the gross phrase, a knight,) that swaggers in the street, and, being taken, has no money in his purse to pay for his fees, it shall be a part of your duty to intreat me to let him go.

1st. Watch. Oh, marvellous! are there such chevaliers?

2nd. Watch. Some two hundred; that's the least that are revealed.

[Mendosa groans.

Captain. What groan is that? Bring a light! Who lies there?
It is the Lord Mendosa, kinsman to our Duke.
Speak, good my lord! relate your dire mischance!
Life, like a fearful servant, flies his master;
Art must atone[38] them, or the whole man's lost.
Convey him to a surgeon's, then return;
No place shall be unsearch'd, until we find
The truth of this mischance; make haste again.

---

[36] A "gingling spur" seems to have been an article upon which the gallants of two centuries ago greatly prided themselves. Many allusions to this species of foppery might be adduced, but, I shall content myself with quoting one only. In Middleton's "More Dissemblers Besides Women," the *Captain of the Gipsies*, enumerating the articles stolen by his gang, mentions

"Shirts or napkins, smocks or towels,

"Boots, or spurs with gingling rowels."

[37] A halberd was the common weapon of a *London* watchman in Marston's time; and, as has before been observed, he, in common with most of his cotemporary dramatists, introduces English customs, and even slang expressions, where we should least expect to meet with them.

[38] Atone is sometimes used by old writers in the sense of to reconcile, or reunite.—"Nay, if he had been cool enough to tell us that, there had been some hope to *atone* you."—*Jonson's* "*Silent Woman,*" *Act IV.*

[*Part of the Watch bear of* Mendosa.

Whose house is this stands open? In, and search
What guests that house contains, and bring them forth.

[*The remainder of the Watch enter the houses of* Claridiana *and* Mizaldus.

This nobleman's misfortune stirs my quiet,
And fills my soul with fearful fantasies;
But, I'll unwind this labyrinth of doubt,
Else industry shall lose part of self's labour.

(*Re-enter the Watch, with* Claridiana *and* Mizaldus,
*taken in one another's houses, in their shirts
and night-gowns. They see one another.*[39]

Who have we there? Signors, cannot you tell us
How our Prince's kinsman came wounded to the death
Nigh to your houses?

Miz. (*To* Cla.) Hey-day! Cross-Ruff at midnight! Is't Christmas, you go a gaming to your neighbour's house?[40]

Cla. Dost make a mummer of me, ox-ahead?

Captain. Make answer, gentlemen, it doth concern you.

Miz. "Ox-head" will bear an action. I'll ha' the law; I'll not be yok'd. Bear witness, gentlemen, he calls me ox-head.

Captain. Do you hear, sir?

Cla. Very well, very well; take law, and hang thyself; I care not. Had she no other but that good face to doat upon? I'd rather she had dealt with a dangerous Frenchman, than with such a Pagan.

Captain. Are you mad? Answer my demand!

Miz. I am as good a Christian as thyself, though my wife have now new christen'd me.

Captain. Are you deaf, you make no answer?

Cla. Would I had had the circumcising of thee, Jew! I'd ha' cut short your cuckold-maker; I would i'faith! I would i'faith!

---

[39] The 4to. 1631, wholly omits this Stage-Direction.

[40] Marston had an *English* Christmas in his thoughts, when he wrote this passage. It is still customary in some of the Northern Counties, for young men and women, on, Christmas Eve, to change clothes, and visit their neighbours' houses; when they amuse themselves with mumming and various gambols.

Captain. Away with them to prison; they'll answer better there.

Miz. Not too fast, gentlemen! What's our crime?

Captain. Murder of the Duke's kinsman, Signor Mendosa.

Cla. & *Miz*. Nothing else? We did it! we did it! we did it!

Captain. Take heed, gentlemen, what you confess.

Cla. I'll confess anything, since I am made a fool of by a knave. I'll be hang'd like an innocent, that's flat.

Miz. I'll not see my shame; hemp instead of a quacksalver! You shall put out mine eyes, and my head shall be bought to make ink-horns of.

Captain. You do confess the murder?

Cla. Sir, 'tis true—
Done by a faithless Christian and a Jew.

Captain. To prison with them; we will hear no further;
The tongue betrays the heart of guilty murther.

[Exeunt.

SCENE 2.—*Pavie.—A Room in the* Countess' *House.*

Enter ROGERO, *the* COUNTESS, *and* ANNA.

Rog. Welcome to Pavia, sweet; and, may this kiss
Chase melancholy from thy company.
Speak, my soul's joy, how fare you, after travel?

Countess. Like one that scapeth danger on the seas,
Yet trembles with cold fears, being safe on land,
With bare imagination of what's past.

Rog. Fear keep with cowards! air-stars cannot move!

Countess. Fear in this kind, my lord, doth sweeten love.

Rog. To think fear joy, dear, I cannot conjecture.

Countess. Fear's sire to fervency, which makes love's sweet prove nectar.
Trembling desire, fear, hope, and doubtful leisure,
Distil from love the quintessence of pleasure.

Rog. Madam, I yield to you; fear keeps with love.
My oratory is too weak against you;
You have the ground of knowledge, wise experience,

51

Which makes your argument invincible.

    Countess. You are time's scholar, and can flatter weakness.

    Rog. Custom allows it; and we plainly see,

Princes and women maintain flattery.

    Countess. Anna, go see my jewels and my trunks. Be aptly placed in their several rooms.

[Exit Anna.

Enter GNIACA.

My lord, know you this gallant? 'tis a complete gentleman.

    Rog. I do; 'tis Count Gniaca, my endeared friend.

    Gniaca. Welcome to Pavie; welcome, fairest lady!

Your sight, dear friend, is life's restorative;

This day's the period of long-wish'd content,

More welcome to me, than day to the world,

Night to the wearied, or gold to a miser:

Such joy feels friendship in society.

    Countess. A rare-shap'd man, compare them both together.

    Rog. Our loves are friendly twins, both at a birth;

The joy you taste, that joy do I conceive;

This day's the jubilee of my desire.

    Countess. He's fairer than he was when first I saw him;

This little time makes him more excellent.

    Gniaca. Relate some news; hark you, what lady's that?

Be open-breasted, so will I to thee.   [*They whisper.*

    Countess. (Aside.) Error did blind him, that did paint love blind,

For my love plainly judges difference.

Love is clear-sighted, and with eagle's eyes,

Undazzled, looks upon bright sun-beam'd beauty

Nature did rob herself, when she made him,

Blushing to see her work excel herself.

'Tis shape makes mankind femelacy.

Forgive me, Rogero, it is my fate

To love thy friend, and 'quite thy love with hate.

I must enjoy him! let hope thy passions smother;

52

Faith can't cool blood; I'll clip him, wer't my brother;
Such is the heat of my sincere affection;
Hell nor earth can keep love in subjection.

    Gniaca. (*To Countess.*) I crave your honour, that my ignorance
Of what you were, may gain a courteous pardon.

    Countess. There needs no pardon, where there's no offence.—
(*Aside.*) His tongue strikes music, ravishing my sense;
I must be sudden, else desire confounds me.

    Rog. What sport affords this climate for delight?

    Gniaca. We'll hawk and hunt to-day; as for to-morrow,
Variety shall feed variety.

    Countess. Dissimulation women's armour is;
Aid love, belief, and female constancy!   [*Aside.*
Oh, I am sick, my lord! Kind Rogero, help me!

    Rog. Forfend it, heav'n! Madam, sit; how fare you?
My life's best comfort, speak; oh, speak, sweet saint!

    Countess. Fetch art to keep life! run, my love, I faint!
My vital blood[41] runs coldly through my veins;
I see lean Death, with eyes imaginary,
Stand fearfully before me. Here my end,
A wife unconstant, yet thy loving friend!

    Rog. As swift as thought, fly I to wish[42] thee aid.

                                       [*Exit.*

    Countess: Thus innocence by craft is soon betray'd.
My lord Gniaca, 'tis your art must heal me;
I'm love-sick for your love! love, love, for loving!
I blush for speaking truth; fair sir, believe me,
Beneath the moon nought but your frown can grieve me.

    Gniaca. Lady, by heaven, me think's this fit is strange.

    Countess. Count not my love light, for this sudden change.
By Cupid's bow I swear, and will avow,
I never knew true perfect love till now.

    Gniaca. Wrong not yourself, me, and your dearest friend;

---

[41] The 4tos. read, "my vital *breath.*"

[42] To *wish* is an obsolete verb, signifying to ask or require.

Your love is violent, and soon will end.
Love is not love, unless love doth persever;
That love is perfect love, that loves for ever.
    Countess. Such love is mine, believe it, well-shaped youth;
Though women use to lie, yet I speak truth.
Give sentence for my life or speedy death:—
Can you affect me?
    Gniaca. I should belie my thoughts, to give denial;
But then, to friendship I must turn disloyal.
I will not wrong my friend, let that suffice.
    Countess. I'll be a miracle; for love; a woman dies!

[Offers to stab herself.

    Gniaca. Hold, madam, these are soul-killing passions;
I'd rather wrong my friend, than you yourself.
    Countess. Love me, or else, by Jove, death's but delay'd!
My vow is fix'd in heav'n; fear shall not move me;
My life is death with tortures, 'less you love me.
    Gniaca. Give me some respite, and I will resolve you.
    Countess. My heart denies it.
My blood is violent; now, or else never.
Love me; and, like Love's Queen, I'll fall before thee,
Inticing dalliance from thee with my smiles,
And steal thy heart with my delicious kisses.
I'll study art in love; that, in a rapture,
Thy soul shall taste pleasures excelling nature.
Both art and nature, in large recompense,
Shall be profuse in ravishing thy sense.
    Gniaca. You have prevail'd; I'm your's from all the world;
Thy wit and beauty have entranc'd my soul.
I long for dalliance; my blood burns like fire:
Hell's pain on earth is to delay desire.
    Countess. I kiss thee for that breath. This day you hunt;
In midst of all your sports, leave you Rogero;
Return to me, whose life rests in thy sight,
Where pleasure shall make nectar our delight.

54

Gniaca. I condescend to what thy will implores me:
He, that but now neglected thee, adores thee.
But, see, here comes my friend; fear makes him tremble.
Countess. Women are witless, that cannot dissemble.

Re-enter ROGERO, *with a* DOCTOR *and* ANNA.

Now I am sick again; where's my lord Rogero?
His love and my health's vanish'd both together.
Rog. Wrong not thy friend, dear friend, in thy extremes;
Here's a profound Hippocrates, my dear,
To minister to thee the spirit of health.
Countess. Your sight to me, my lord, excels all physic;
I'm better, far, my love, than when you left me;
Your friend was comfortable to me at the last;
'Twas but a fit, my lord, and now 'tis past.
Are all things ready, sir?
Anna. Yes, madam, the house is fit.
Gniaca. Desire in women is the life of wit.

[*Exeunt*.

SCENE 3.—*Venice.*—Claridiana's *House.*

Enter ABIGAIL *and* THAIS, *at opposite doors.*

Abig. Oh, partner, I am with child of laughter, and none but you can be my midwife. Was there ever such a game at noddy![43]

Thais. Our husbands think they are foremen of the jury; they hold the heretic point of predestination, and are sure they are born to be hanged.

Abig. They are like to prove men, of judgment; but, for killing of him that's yet alive, and well nigh recovered.

Thais. As soon as my man saw the watch come up, all his spirit was down.

---

[43] The game now called Cribbage.—"Mine host's policy for the drawing guests to his house, and keeping them when he had them, is farre more ingenious than our duller ways of Billiards, Kettle Pins, Noddy Boards, &c."—*Gayton's Festivous Notes on Don Quixote.*

55

Abig. But, though they have made us good sport in speech, they did hinder us of good sport in action. Oh, wench, imagination is strong in pleasure.

Thais. That's true; for the opinion my good man had of enjoying you, made him do wonders.

Abig. Why should a weak man, that is so soon satisfied, desire variety?

Thais. Their answer is, to feed on pheasants continually, would breed a loathing.

Abig. Then, if we seek for strange flesh, that have stomachs at will, 'tis pardonable.

Thais. Ay, if men had any feeling of it; but they judge us by themselves.

Abig. Well, we will bring them to the gallows, and then, like kind virgins, beg their lives, and after live at our pleasures, and this bridle shall still rein them.

Thais. Faith, if we were disposed, we might sin[44] as safe as if we had the broad seal to warrant it: but, that night's work will stick by me this forty weeks. Come, shall we go visit the discontented Lady Lentulus, whom the Lord Mendosa has confessed to his chirurgeon he would have robbed? I thought great men would but have robbed the poor, yet he, the rich.

Abig. He thought that the richer purchase,[45] though with the worse conscience. But, we'll to comfort her, and then go hear our husbands' lamentations. They say, mine has compiled an ungodly volume of Satires against women, and call his book *The Snarl*.

Thais. But, he's in hope his book will save him?

Abig. God defend that it should; or any that snarl in that fashion.

Thais. Well, wench, if I could be metamorphosed into thy shape, I should have my husband pliant to me in his life, and soon rid of him: for, being weary with his continual motion, he'd die of a consumption.

Abig. Make much of him, for all our wanton prize;
Follow the proverb,—*Merry be, and wise!*

[*Exeunt.*

---

[44] The 4tos. read,—"We might *seem* as safe."

[45] *Purchase* is an obsolete cant term for stolen articles. In "Henry V." Act III. Scene 2, the *Boy* says of *Nym*, *Bardolph*, and *Pistol*, "They will steal anything, and call it *purchase*."

SCENE 4.—*Pavia.—A Room in the* Countess' *House.*

Enter the COUNTESS *and* ANNA.

Countess. Time, that devourest all mortality,
Run swiftly these few hours,
And bring Gniaca on thy aged shoulders,
That I may clip the rarest model of
Creation. Do this, gentle Time!
And I will curl thine aged silver lock,
And dally with thee in delicious pleasure!
Medea-like, I will renew thy youth;
But, if thy frozen steps delay my love,
I'll poison thee with murder, curse thy paths,
And make thee know a time of infamy.
Anna, give watch, and bring me certain notice
When Count Gniaca doth approach my house.
Anna. Madam, I go.—
I'm kept for pleasure, though I never taste it;
For, 'tis the usher's office still to cover
His lady's private meetings with her lover.

[Aside and Exit.

Countess. Desire, thou quenchless flame, that burn'st our souls,
Cease to torment me!
The dew of pleasure shall put out thy fire,
And quite consume thee with satiety.
Lust shall be cool'd with lust; wherein I'll prove,
The life of love is only sav'd by love.

Re-enter ANNA.

Anna. Madam, he's coming.
Countess. Thou blessed Mercury!
Prepare a banquet, fit to please the gods!
Let sphere-like music breathe delicious tones
Into our mortal ears! perfume the house

57

With odoriferous scents, sweeter than myrrh,
Or all the spices in Panchaia!   [*Exit* Anna.
His sight and touching we will recreate,
That his five senses shall be five-fold happy.
His breath, like roses, casts out sweet perfume;
Time now with pleasure shall itself consume.

Enter GNIACA *in his hunting-weeds.*

How like Adonis in his hunting-weeds
Looks this same goddess-tempter!
And art thou come! this kiss entrance[46] thy soul!
Gods, I don't envy you, for, know you this,
Ways here on earth complete excel your bliss;
I'll not change this night's pleasure with you all.
    Gniaca. Thou creature, made by Love, compos'd of pleasure,
That mak'st true use of thy creation,
In thee both wit and beauty's resident,
Delightful pleasure, unpeer'd excellence.
This is the fate fix'd fast unto thy birth,
That thou alone should'st be man's heav'n on earth;
If I alone may but enjoy thy love,
I'll not change earthly joy, to be heav'n's Jove;
For though that women-haters now are common,
They all shall know earth's joy consists in woman.
    Countess. My love was dotage till I loved thee,
For thy soul truly tastes our petulance.
Condition's lover, Cupid's intelligencer,
That makes men understand what pleasure is:
These are fit tributes unto thy knowledge;
For, women's beauty o'er men bears that rule,
Our power commands the rich, the wise, the fool.
Though scorn grows big in man, in growth and stature,
Yet women are the rarest works of nature.

---

[46] The 4to. 1631 reads, "*enters into* thy soul."

58

Gniaca. I do confess the truth, and must admire
That, women can command rare man's desire.

(Music; and a banquet is brought in.)

Countess. Cease admiration, sit to Cupid's feast,
The preparation to Paphéon dalliance.
Harmonious music, breathe thy silver airs,
To stir up appetite to Venus' banquet,
That breath of pleasure, that entrances souls,
Making that instant happiness a heaven,
In the true taste of love's deliciousness.
Gniaca. Thy words are able to stir cold desire[47]
Into his flesh that lies intomb'd in ice,
Having lost the feeling use of warmth in blood;
Then, how much more in me, whose youthful veins,
Like a proud river, overflow their bounds!
Pleasure's ambrosia, or love's nourisher;
I long for privacy; come, let us in;
'Tis custom, and not reason, makes love sin.
Countess. I'll lead the way to Venus' paradise,
Where thou shalt taste that fruit that made man wise.

[Exit.

Gniaca. Sing notes of pleasure, to elate our blood!
Why should heav'n frown on joys that do us good?
I come, Isabella, keeper of love's treasure,
To force thy blood to lust, and ravish pleasure.

[Exit.

(After some short song,[48] enter the COUNTESS *and* GNIACA *again, she
hanging about his neck lasciviously.)*

---

[47] "*Cold* desire" appears to be a somewhat contradictory expression, but I have not deemed it advisable to make any alteration.

[48] These *Songs* are seldom met with in the old plays. The choice of one was probably left to the discretion of the singer.

Gniaca. Still I'm thy captive, yet my thoughts are free:
To be love's bondsman is true liberty.
I've swum in seas of pleasure without ground:
Vent'rous desire, past depth, itself hath drown'd.
Such skill hath beauty's art in a true lover,
That dead desire to life it can recover;
Thus beauty our desire can soon advance,
Then straight again kill it with dalliance.
Divinest women, your enchanting breaths
Give lovers many lives and many deaths!
Countess. May thy desire to me for ever last,
Not die by surfeit on my delicates;
And, as I tie this jewel 'bout th'y neck,
So may I tie thy constant love to mine,
Never to seek weaking variety,
That greedy curse of man, and woman's hell,
Where nought but shame and loath'd diseases dwell.
Gniaca. You counsel well, dear lady learn it, then;
For, change is given more to you than men.
Countess. My faith to thee, like rocks, shall never move;
The sun shall change his course, ere I my love.

Re-enter ANNA.

Anna. Madam, the Count Rogero knocks.
Countess. Dear love, into my chamber, till I send
My hate from sight.
Gniaca. Lust makes me wrong my friend.

[*Exit.*

Countess. Anna, stand here, and entertain Rogero;
I, from my window, straight will give him answer.
The serpent's wit to woman rest in me;
By that man fell; then, why not he by me?
Feign'd sighs and tears, dropp'd from a woman's eye,
Blind man of reason, strike his knowledge dumb;
Wit arms a woman; Count Rogero, come!

60

[Exit.

Anna. My office still is under; yet, in time
Ushers prove masters: degrees make us climb.

(Rogero knocks.)

Who knocks? is't you, my noble lord?

Enter ROGERO, in his hunting-weeds.

Rog. Came my friend hither, Count Gniaca?
Anna. No, my good lord.
Rog. Where's my Isabella?
Anna. In her chamber.
Rog. Good! I'll visit her.
Anna. The chamber's lock'd, my lord; she will be private.
Rog. Lock'd against me, my saucy malapert?
Anna. Be patient, good my lord; she'll give you answer.
Rog. Isabella, life of love, speak! 'tis I that call.

(The Countess appears at a Window.)[49]

Countess. I must desire your lordship pardon me.
Rog. Lordship! what's this? Isabella, art thou blind?
Countess. My lust was blind, but now my soul's clear -sighted,
And sees the spots that did corrupt my flesh:
Those tokens sent from hell, brought by desire,
The messengers of everlasting death.
   Anna. My lady's in her pulpit, now she'll preach.
   Rog. Is not thy lady mad? In verity,
I always took her for a Puritan,
And now she shews it.
   Countess. Mock not repentance; prophanation
Brings mortals laughing to damnation.

---

[49] The respective situations of the parties are not very clearly pointed out here. It appears
as if the *Countess* addressed *Rogero* from the window of an *inner* apartment.

61

Believe it, lord, Isabella's ill-past life,
Like gold refin'd, shall make a perfect wife.
I stand on firm ground now, before on ice;
We know not virtue, till we taste of vice.

 Rog. Do you hear, dissimulation, woman, sinner?

 Countess. Leave my house, good my lord; and, for my part,
I look for a most wished reconciliation
Betwixt myself and my most wronged husband;
Tempt not contrition, then, religious lord.

 Rog. Indeed, I was one of your family once; but, do not I know these are but brain-tricks, and where the devil has the fee simple, he will keep possession; and will you halt before me, that yourself has made a cripple?

 Countess. Nay, then, you wrong me; and, disdained lord,
I paid thee for thy pleasures vendible,
Whose mercenary flesh I bought with coin;
I will divulge thy baseness, 'less with speed
Thou leave my house and my society.

 Rog. Already turn'd apostate! but now all pure;
Now damn'd your faith is; and your loves endure
Like dew upon the grass; when pleasure's sun
Shines on your virtues, all your virtue's done.
I'll leave thy house and thee; go, get thee in,
Thou gaudy child of pride, and nurse of sin.

 Countess. Rail not on me, my lord, for if you do,
My hot desire of vengeance shall strike wonder:
Revenge in woman falls like dreadful thunder.

[Exit.

 Anna. Your lordship will command me do farther service?

 Rog. I thank thee for thy watchful service past,
Thy usher-like attendance on the stairs,
Being true signs of thy humility.

 Anna. I hope I did discharge my place with care.

 Rog. Ushers should have much wit, but little hair;
Thou hast of both sufficient; pr'ythee, leave me;
If thou hast an honest lady, commend me to her;

But, she is none.   [*Exit* Anna.
Farewell, thou private strumpet, worse than common!
Man were on earth an angel, but for woman:
That seven-fold branch of hell from them doth grow;
Pride, Lust, and Murder they raise from below,
With all their fellow sins. Women are made
Of blood, without souls; when their beauties fade,
And their lust's past, av'rice or bawdry
Makes them still lov'd; then they buy venery,
Bribing damnation, and hire brothel slaves:
Shame's their executors, infamy their graves.
Your painting will wipe off, which art did hide,
And shew your ugly shape, in spite of pride.
Farewell, Isabella, poor in soul and fame,
I leave thee rich in nothing but in shame.
Then, soul-less women, know, whose faiths are hollow,
Your lust being quench'd, a bloody act must follow.
                                                             [*Exit*.

END OF ACT III.

ACT IV.

SCENE 1.—*Venice.*—*The Senate House.*

Enter DUKE AMAGO *and* SENATORS, *with the Captain of the Watch and his Men.*

Duke. Justice, that makes princes like the gods, Draws us unto the Senate,
That with unpartial balance we may poise
The crimes and innocence of all offenders;
Our presence can chase bribery from laws:
He best can judge, that hears himself the cause.
 1st. Senator. True, mighty Duke; it best becomes our places
To have our light from you, the sun of virtue.
Subject authority, for gain, love, or fear,
Oft 'quits the guilty, and condemns the clear.
 Duke. The land and people's mine; the crime being known,
I must redress: my subjects' wrong's mine own.
Call for the two, suspected for the murder
Of Mendosa, our endeared kinsman;
These voluntary murd'rers, that confess
The murder of him that is yet alive.
We'll sport with serious justice for a while;
In shew, we'll frown on them that make us smile.
 2nd. Senator. Bring forth the pris'ners, we may hear their answers.

(Officers bring in Claridiana *and* Mizaldus.*)*

Duke. Stand forth, you vipers, that have suck'd the blood,
And lopp'd a branch sprung from a royal tree!
What can you answer, to escape from tortures?
 Miz. We have confess'd the act to God and man,
Our ghostly father, and that worthy captain:
We beg not life, but favourable death.
 Duke. On what ground sprung your hate to him we lov'd?

Cla. Upon that curse laid on Venetian jealousy. We thought he, being a courtier, would have made us Magnificos of the right stamp, and have play'd at Primero[50] in the Presence,[51] with gold of the city, brought from our Indies.

Miz. Nay, more, my lord; we feared that your kinsman, for a mess of sonnets, would have given the plot of us and our wives to some needy poet; and, for sport and profit, brought us, in some Venetian comedy, upon the stage.

Duke. Our justice dwells with mercy; be not desp'rate!

1st. Senator. His highness fain would save your lives, if you would see it.

Miz. All the law in Venice shall not save me; I will not be saved.

Miz. (To Cla.) Fear not! I have a trick to bring us to hanging, in spite of the law.

Cla. Why, now I see thou lovest me; thou hast confirmed thy friendship to me for ever by these words. Why, I should never hear lanthorn and candle called for, but I should think it was for me and my wife. I'll hang for that. Forget not thy trick! Upon 'em with thy trick I long for sentence.

2nd. Senator. Will you appeal for mercy to the Duke?

Cla. Kill not thy justice, Duke, to save our lives! We have deserved death.

Miz. Make us not precedents for after wrongs. I will receive punishment for my sins, it shall be a means to lift me towards heaven.

Cla. Let's have our desert; we crave no favour.

Duke. Take 'em asunder!—Grave justice makes us mirth:
The man is soul-less that ne'er smiles[52] on earth.

[Mizaldus *is led out.*
Signor Claridiana, relate the weapon you kill'd him with, and the manner.

Cla. My lord, your lustful kinsman (I can call him no better) came sneaking to my house, like a promoter[53] to spy flesh in Lent. Now, I, having a Venetian

---

[50] A game at cards, which, from the continual mention of it made by the old dramatists, must have been a great favourite of our ancestors. Sir J. Harrington has left what he calls an Epigram, of fifty lines, entitled "The Story of Marcus' Life at Primero," from which some confused idea of the nature of the game may be gathered.—Minshieu thus explains the word: "*Primero* and *Primavista*, two games at cards. *Primum, et primum visum*, that is, the first, and first seen; because, he that first can shew such an order of cards, wins the game."

[51] The Presence-Chamber.

[52] The 4tos. read, "*sins*" on earth.

[53] An Informer.

spirit, watch'd my time, and, with my rapier, ran him through, knowing all pains are but trifles, to the horn of a citizen.

Duke. Take him aside!

(They lead out Claridiana, *and bring in* Mizaldus.*)*

Signior Mizaldus, what weapon had you for this bloody act? What dart used death?

Miz. My lord, I brain'd him with a lever, my neighbour lent me; and he stood by, and cried, "Strike home, old boy!"

Duke. With several instruments!—Bring them face to face!

[Claridiana *is brought in.*

With what killed you our nephew?

Cla. With a rapier, liege.

Miz. 'Tis a lie! I kill'd him with a lever, and thou stood'st by.

Cla. Dost think to save me, and hang thyself? No, I scorn it. Is this the trick thou said'st thou had'st? I kill'd him, Duke; he only gave consent; 'twas I that did it.

Miz. Thou hast always been cross to me, and wilt be to my death. Have I taken all these pains to bring thee to hanging, and dost thou slip now?

Cla. We shall never agree in a tale, till we come to the gallows; then we shall jump.

Miz. I'll shew you a cross-point, if you cross me thus, when thou shalt not see it.

Cla. I'll make a wry mouth at that, or it shall cost me a fall. 'Tis thy pride to be hang'd alone, because thou scorn'st my company; but it shall be known I am as good a man as thyself, and in these actions will keep company with thy betters, Jew.

Miz. Monster!

Cla. Dog-killer!

Miz. Fencer! [*They bustle.*

Duke. Part 'em! part 'em!

Miz. Hang us, and quarter us! we shall never be parted till then.

Duke. You do confess the murther done by both?

Cla. But that I would not have the slave laugh at me, and count me a coward, I have a very good mind to live; but, I am resolute; 'tis but a turn. *(Aside.)* —— I do confess.

Miz. So do I.
Pronounce our doom; we are prepared to die.

Duke. We sentence you to hang till you be dead.
Since you were men eminent in place and worth,
We give a christian burial to you both.[54]

Cla. Not in one grave together, we beseech you! we shall ne'er agree.

Miz. He scorns my company till the day of judgment. I'll not hang with him!

Duke. You hang together, that shall make you friends:
An everlasting hatred death soon ends.
To prison with them, till the day of death!
King's words, like fate, must never change their breath.

Miz. You malice-monger, I'll be hanged afore thee, an't be but to vex thee.

Cla. I'll do you as good a turn, or the hangman and I shall fall out.

[Exeunt ambo, guarded.

Duke. Now to our kinsman, shame to royal blood;
Bring him before us.

(The Captain of the Watch fetches in MENDOSA,
in his night-gown and cap, guarded.)

Theft in a prince is sacrilege to honour;
'Tis virtue's scandal, death of royalty;
I blush to see my shame. Nephew, sit down.—
Justice, that smiles on those, on him must frown—

(Aside.

Speak freely, Captain, where found you him wounded?

Captain. Between the Widow's house and these cross neighbours'. Besides, an artificial ladder, made of ropes, was fastened to her window, which he

---

[54] The 4tos. assign this speech to the 1*st. Senator;* but It seems to belong rather to the *Duke,* to whom I have accordingly restored it.

confess'd he brought, to rob her of jewels and coin. My knowledge yields no
farther circumstance.

Duke. Thou know'st too much! Would I were past all knowledge,
I might forget my grief springs from my shame!—
Thou monster, of my blood, answer in brief
To these assertions, made against thy life!
Is thy soul guilty of so base a fact?

Men. I do confess I did intend to rob her;
In the attempt, I fell, and hurt myself.—
Law's thunder, is but death; I dread it not,
So my Lentulus' honour be preserv'd
From black suspicion of a lustful night.   [*Aside.*

Duke. Thy head's thy forfeit for thy heart's offence.
Thy blood's prerogative may claim that favour.
Thy person, then to death's doom'd by just laws;
Thy death is infamous, but worse the cause.

[*Exeunt.*

SCENE 2.—*Pavia.*—*Enter the* COUNTESS, *followed by* GNIACA.

Countess: O heav'ns, that I was born to be hate's slave;
The food of rumour, that devours my fame!
I'm call'd Insatiate Countless, lust's paramour,
A glorious devil, and the noble whore.
I'm sick, vex'd, and tormented. Oh, revenge!

Gniaca. On whom would Isabella be reveng'd?

Countess. Upon a viper, that does soil mine honour;
I will not name him, till I be reveng'd.
See, here's the libels are divulg'd against me,
An everlasting scandal to my name;
And thus the villain writes, to my disgrace:

(*She reads.*)

"Who loves ISABELLA, the insatiate,
    "Needs Atlas' back for to content her lust;

68

"That wand'ring strumpet, and chaste wedlock's hate,
    "That renders back deceit, for loyal trust;[55]
"That sacrilegious thief to Hymen's rites,
    "Making her lust her god; heav'n, her de lights."
Swell not, proud heart! I'll quench thy grief in blood:
Desire in woman cannot be withstood.
    Gniaca. I'll be thy champion, sweet, 'gainst all the world;
Name but the villain that defames thee thus.
    Countess. Dare thy hand execute whom my tongue condemns?
Then thou art truly valiant, mine for ever;
But, if thou faint'st, hate must our true love sever.
    Gniaca. By my dead father's soul, my mother's virtues,
And by my knighthood and gentility,
I'll be reveng'd upon the author of
Your obloquy! Name him.
    Countess. Rogero.
    Gniaca. Ha!
    Countess. What! does his name affright thee, coward lord?—
Be mad, Isabella! curse on thy revenge!
This lord was knighted for his father's worth,
Not for his own.
Farewell, thou perjur'd man! I'll leave you all;
You all conspire to work mine honour's fall.
    Gniaca. Stay, Isabella; were he my father's son,
Compos'd of me, he dies,
Delight still keep with thee. Go in.
    Countess. Thou'rt just;
Revenge to me is sweeter now than lust.   [*Exit.*

---

[55] In the 4tos. this line runs as follows:—

    "That renders truth deceit for loyal trust."

From this I could extract no meaning, and I therefore ventured upon a slight alteration. I, however, suspect that the line was originally a "needless Alexandrine," and that a word has been lost by the printer. Perhaps it should stand thus:

    "That renders lies, for truth; deceit, for loyal trust."

(Enter ROGERO; *they see one another, and draw, and make a pass.
Then enter* ANNA.*)*

Anna. What mean you, nobles, will you kill each other?
Rog. and *Gniaca.* Hold!
Rog. Thou shame to friendship, what intends thy hate?
Gniaca. Love arms my hand, makes my sword valiant;
Isabel's wrongs now sit upon my sword,
To fall more heavy on thy coward head,
Than thunderbolts upon Jove's rifted oaks.
Deny thy scandal, or defend thy life!
Rog. What! have thy faith and reason left thee both,
That thou art only flesh, without a soul?
Hast thou no feeling of thyself and me?
Blind rage, that will not let thee see thyself!
Gniaca. I come not to dispute, but execute;
And thus comes death.—

(Another pass.)

Rog. And thus I break her dart.
Here's at thy whore's face!
Gniaca. 'Tis miss'd; here's at thy heart!
Stay, let us breathe.
Rog. Let reason govern rage, yet let us leave;
Although most wrong be mine, I can forgive;
In this attempt thy shame will ever live.
Gniaca. Thou'st wrong'd the phœnix, of all women rarest;
She that's most wise, most loving, chaste, and fairest.
Rog. Thou dot'st upon a devil, not a woman,
That has bewitch'd thee with her sorcery,
And drown'd thy soul in Lethe faculties;
Her quenchless lust has quite benumb'd thy knowledge;
Thy intellectual powers oblivion smothers,
That thou art nothing but forgetfulness.
Gniaca. What's this to Isabel? my sin's my own,

Her faults were none, until thou mad'st 'em known.

 Rog. Leave her, and leave thy shame where first thou found'st it!
Else live a bondslave to diseased lust,
Devoured in her gulf-like appetite,
And infamy shall write thy epitaph;
Thy memory leave nothing but thy crimes,
A scandal to thy name in future times.

 Gniaca. Put up your weapon, I dare hear you further;
Insatiate lust is still the sire murther.

 Rog. Believe it, friend, if her heart-blood were vext,
Though you kill me, new pleasure makes you next;
She lov'd me dearer than she loves you now;
She'll ne'er be faithful, has twice broke her vow.
This curse pursues female adultery,
They'll swim through blood for sin's variety;
Their pleasure's like a sea, groundless and wide:
A woman's lust was never satisfied.

 Gniaca. Fear whispers in my breast, I have a soul
That blushes red, for 'tending bloody facts.
Forgive me, friend, if I can be forgiven!
Thy counsel is the path leads me to heaven.

 Rog. I do embrace thy reconciled love—

 Gniaca. That death or danger now shall ne'er remove.—
Go, tell thy insatiate Countess, Anna,
We have escap'd the shares of her false love,
Vowing for ever to abandon her.

 Rog. You've heard our resolution; pray be gone!

 Anna. My office ever rested at your pleasure;
I was the Indian, yet you had the treasure.
My faction often sweats, and oft takes cold;
Then gild true diligence o'er with gold!

 Rog. Thy speech deserves it; there is gold;
Be honest now, and not love's noddy,[56]

---

[56] I confess that I do not understand this passage. A *noddy* is a simpleton; but there is
apparently some allusion to the game of that name. (*Vide Note* 43.)

Turn'd up and play'd on, while thou keep'st the stock!
Pr'ythee, let's ha' thy absence.

    Anna. Lords, farewell!

[Exit.

    Rog. 'Tis whores and panders that make earth like hell.

    Gniaca. Now I am got out of lust's labyrinth,
I will to Venice for a certain time,
To recreate my much-abused spirits,
And then revisit Pavie and my friend.

    Rog. I'll bring you on your way, but must return;
Love is like Etna, and will ever burn;
Yet, now desire is quench'd, flam'd once in height:
Till man knows hell he never has firm faith.

[Exeunt.

Enter the COUNTESS, raving,[57] and ANNA.

    Countess. Out, screech-owl, messenger of my revenge's death;
Thou dost bely Gniaca; 'tis not so!

    Anna. Upon mine honesty, they are united.

    Countess. Thy honesty, thou vassal to my pleasure!
Take that!   [Strikes her.
Dar'st thou controul me when that I say no?
Art not my footstool? did not I create thee,
And make thee gentle, being born a beggar?
Thou'st been my woman's pander for a crown,
And dost thou stand upon thy honesty?

    Anna. I'm what you please, madam; yet 'tis so.

    Countess. Slave, I will slit thy tongue, 'less thou say'st no.

    Anna. No, no, no, madam!

    Countess. I'll have my humour, though they now be false.
Faint-hearted coward, get thee from my sight!

---

[57] The 4to. 1631 reads, "Enter the Countess running."

When, villain?[58] Haste, and come not near me!

    Anna. Madam, I run.—Her sight like death doth fear me.

[Aside and Exit.

    Countess. Perfidious cowards, stain of nobility!

Venetians, and be reconcil'd with words!

Oh, that I had Gniaca once more here,

Within this prison, made of flesh and bone,

I'd not trust thunder with my fell revenge,

But mine own hands should do the dire exploit,

And fame should chronicle a woman's acts.

My rage respects the persons, not the facts;

Their place and worth hath power to defame me;

Mean hate is stingless, and does only name me;

I not regard it, 'tis high blood that swells:

Give me revenge, and damn me into hells!

Enter DON SAGO, a Colonel, with a band of Soldiers, and a
LIEUTENANT.

A gallant Spaniard,[59] I will hear him speak;

Grief must be speechless, ere the heart can break.

    Don Sago. Lieutenant, let good discipline be us'd,

In quart'ring of our troops into the city;

Not separated into many streets,

That shews weak love, but not sound policy.

Disunion in small numbers, makes all weak;

Forces united are the nerves of war,

Mother and nurse of observation.

---

[58] The use of the word *when*, to express impatience, was formerly universal. See an instance in "Julius Cæsar," Act ii. Scene 1.

"Lucius, I say!—

"I would it were my fault to sleep so soundly.—

"*When*, Lucius, *when?*"

[59] The time of action of this Play appears to be 1525, after the defeat of Francis the 1st. by Charles the 5th, at Pavia.

73

Whose rare ingenious spright[60] fills all the world,
By looking on itself with piercing eyes,
Will look through strangers' imbecilities;
Therefore, be careful.

    Lieu. All shall be order'd fitting your command;
For the three gifts which make a soldier rare,
Are love and duty, with a valiant care.

[Exeunt Lieutenant and Soldiers.

    Don Sago. What rarity of women feeds my sight,
And leads my senses in a maze of wonder?
Bellona, thou wert my mistress, till I saw that shape,
But now, my sword I'll consecrate to her,
Leave Mars, and become Cupid's martialist.
Beauty can turn the rugged face of War,
And make him smile upon delightful Peace,
Courting her smoothly, like a femalist.
I grow a slave unto omnipotent Love,
Who changes hearts, and makes our fate remove.

    Countess. Revenge, not pleasure, now o'era-rules my blood;
Rage shall drown faint love in a crimson flood;
And were he caught, I'd make him murder's hand.

    Don Sago. Methinks 'twere joy to die at her command.
I'll speak, to hear her speech, whose pow'rful breath
Is able to infuse life into death.

    Countess. He comes to speak. He's mine! by love, he's mine!

    Don Sago. Lady, think bold intrusion courtesy;
'Tis but imagination alters them;
Then, 'tis your thoughts, not I, that do offend.

    Countess. Sir, your intrusion's yet but courtesy,
Unless your future humour alter it.

    Don Sago. Why, then, divinest woman, know, my soul
Is dedicated to thy shrine of beauty,
To pray for mercy, and repent wrongs

---

[60] i. e. *spirit*. The word, as now written, was long considered in verse as a monosyllable.—
Vide p. 24.

74

Done against love and female purity.
Thou abstract, drawn from nature's empty storehouse,
I am thy slave; command my sword, my heart;
The soul is best tried by the body's smart.

    Countess. You are a stranger to this land and me,
What madness is't for me to trust you, then;
To cozen women is a trade 'mongst men.
Smooth promises, feign'd passion, with a lie,
Deceive our sect[61] of fame and chastity.
What danger durst you hazard for my love?

    Don Sago. Perils that never mortal durst approve.
I'll double all the works of Hercules,
Expose myself in combat 'gainst a host,
Meet danger in a place of certain death,
Yet never shrink, nor give way to my fate.
Bare-breasted meet the murd'rous Tartar's dart,
Or any fatal engine made for death,
Such power has love and beauty from your eye;[62]
He that dies resolute, does never die:
'Tis fear gives death his strength, which if resisted,
Death is but empty air the Fates have twisted.

    Countess. Dare you revenge my quarrel 'gainst a foe?

    Don Sago. Then, ask me if I dare embrace you thus,
Or kiss your hand, or gaze on your bright eye,
Where Cupid dances, or those globes of love.
Fear is my vassal; when I frown, he flies:
A hundred times in life a coward dies.[63]

    Countess. I not suspect your valour, but your will.

    Don Sago. To gain your love, my father's blood I'll spill.

    Countess. Many have sworn the like, yet broke their vow.

    Don Sago. My whole endeavour to your wish shall bow.

---

[61] i.e. *sex.* This word, in its ancient acceptation, is still current amongst the lower orders.

[62] *Sago's* vaunts strongly resemble those of *Claridiana.* Vide p. 24.

[63] This is one of the many imitations of passages in Shakspeare which occur in this Play.—
"Cowards die many times before their deaths," &c. *Julius Cæsar,* Act. ii. Scene 2.

I am your plague, to scourge your enemies.

    Countess. Perform your promise, and enjoy your pleasure,
Spend my love's dowry, that is women's treasure.
But, if thy resolution dread the trial,
I'll tell the world a Spaniard was disloyal.

    Don Sago. Relate your grief; I long to hear their names,
Whose bastard spirit thy true worth defames;
I'll wash thy scandal off with their hearts' bleeds,—
Valour makes difference 'twixt words and deeds.
Tell thy fame's poison; blood shall wash thee white.

    Countess. My spotless honour is a slave to spite.
These are the monsters Venice doth bring forth,
Whose empty souls are bankrupt of true worth:—
False Count Rogero, treach'rous Gniaca,
Counties[64] of Gaza, and of rich Arsena.
Then, if thou beest a knight, help the opprest,
Through danger, safety comes; through trouble, rest;
And so, my love.

    Don Sago. Ignoble villains, their best blood shall prove
Revenge falls heavy that is rais'd by love!

    Countess. Think what reproach is to a woman's name,
Honour'd by birth, by marriage, and by beauty.
Be God on earth, and revenge innocence!
O worthy Spaniard, on my knees I beg,
Forget the persons, think on their offence!

    Don Sago. By the white soul, of honour, by heav'n's Jove,
They die, if their death can attain your love!

    Countess. Thus will I clip thy waist, embrace thee thus,
Thus dally with thy hair, and kiss thee thus.
Our pleasures, Protean-like, in sundry shapes,
Shall with variety stir dalliance.

    Don Sago. I am immortal! O divinest creature,

---

[64] *Count* and *County* were once synonimous. The *County Paris* will occur to every one's recollection; and in Act iv. Scene I. of "Much Ado about Nothing," *Beatrice* speaks of "Princes and *Counties.*"

Thou dost excel the gods in wit and feature!
False Counts, you die! Revenge now shakes his rods:
Beauty condemns you, stronger than the gods.

Countess. Come, Mars of lovers, Vulcan is not here;
Make vengeance like my bed,—quite void of fear.

Don Sago. My senses are entranc'd; and in this slumber,
I taste heav'n's joys, but cannot count the number.

[Exeunt.

SCENE 3.—*Venice.*—Lady Lentulus' *House.*

Enter LADY LENTULUS, ABIGAIL, *and* THAIS.

Abig. Well, madam, you see the destiny that follows marriage; our husbands are quiet now, and must suffer the law.

Thais. If my husband had been worth the begging, some courtier would have had him; he might be begged well enough, for he knows not his own wife from another.

Lady Len. Oh! you're a couple of trusty wenches, to deceive your husbands thus.

Abig. If we had not deceiv'd them, we had been truss'd wenches.

Thais. Our husbands will be hang'd, because they think themselves cuckolds.

Abig. If all true cuckolds were of that mind, the hangman would be the richest occupation; and more wealthy widows, than there be younger brothers to marry them.

Thais. The Merchant-Venturers would be a very small Company.

Abig. 'Tis twelve to one of that; however the rest 'scape, I shall fear a massacre.

Thais. If my husband, hereafter, for his wealth, chance to be dubb'd, I'll have him called the Knight of the Supposed Horn.

Abig. Faith, and it sounds well.

Lady Len. Come, madcaps, leave jesting, and let's deliver them out of their earthly purgation; you are the spirits that torment them; but, my love and lord, kind Mendosa, will lose his life, to preserve mine honour, not for hate to others.

77

Abig. By my troth, if I had been his judge, I should have hang'd him, for having no more wit; I speak as I think, for I would not be hang'd for ne'er a man under the heav'ns.

Thais. Faith, I think I should for my husband: I do not hold the opinion of the philosopher, that writes, we love them best that we enjoy first; for I protest I love my husband better than any that did know me before.

Abig. So do I; yet life and pleasure are two sweet things to a woman.

Lady Len. He that's willing to die to save mine honour, I'll die to save his.

Abig. Tut, believe it who that list, we love a lively man, I grant you; but to maintain that life I'll ne'er consent to die.
This is a rule I still will keep in breast:—
"Love well thy husband, wench, but thyself best!"

Thais. I have followed your counsel hitherto, and mean to do still.

Lady Len. Come, we neglect our business; 'tis no jesting; to-morrow they are executed 'less we reprieve them:
We be their destinies to cast their fate.
Let us all go!

Abig. I fear not to come late.

[Exeunt.

SCENE 4.—Pavia.—A Street.

Enter DON SAGO, with a case of pistols.

Don Sago. Day was my night, and night must be my day;
The sun shined on my pleasure with my love,
And darkness must lend aid to my revenge.
The stage of heaven is hung with solemn black,
A time best fitting to act tragedies.[65]
The night's great queen, that maiden governess,
Musters black clouds to hide her from the world,
Afraid to look on my bold enterprise.
Curs'd creatures, messengers of death, possess the world:

---

[65] It may be necessary to inform some readers, that it was anciently the practice to hang the Stage with black, when a Tragedy was performed.

Night-ravens, screech-owls, and voice-killing mandrakes;[66]
The ghosts of misers, that imprison'd gold
Within the harmless bowels of the earth,
Are night's companions.[67] Bawds to lust and murder,
Be all propitious to my act of justice
Upon the scandalizers of her fame,
That is the life-blood of deliciousness,
Dear Isabella, Cupid's treasurer,
Whose soul contains the richest gifts of love!
Her beauty from my heart fear doth expel;
They relish pleasure best, that dread not hell.

Enter ROGERO.

Who's there?

   Rog. A friend to thee, if thy intents be just and honourable.

   Don Sago. Count Rogero, speak, I am the watch.

   Rog. My name is Rogero; do'st thou know me?

   Don Sago. Yes, sland'rous villain, nurse of obloquy,
Whose poison'd breath has speckled clear-fac'd[68] virtue.
And made a leper of Isabella's fame,
That is as spotless as the eye of heaven.
Thy vital thread's a cutting. Start not, slave!
He's sure of sudden death, heav'n cannot save.

   Rog. Art not Gniaca, turn'd apostata?[69]
Has pleasure once again turn'd thee a devil?
Art not Gniaca, hah?

---

[66] The marvellous properties attributed to the mandrake are very numerous. One of them is, that upon being torn violently from the earth, it utters a lamentable cry, which invariably proves fatal to the rash aggressor.

[67] So in Marlowe's "Jew of Malta:"—

——"Sprites and ghosts that glide by night,
About the place where treasure hath been hid." This is still a popular superstition.

[68] The 4to. 1631, reads "clean-fac'd."

[69] It was once the almost universal practice to write *apostata, statua,* &c. for *apostate, statue,* &c.

79

Don Sago. Oh! that I were, then would I stab myself,
For he is mark'd for death, as well as thee.
I am Don Sago, thy mortal enemy,
Whose hand love makes thy executioner.
    Rog. I know thee, valiant Spaniard, and to thee
Murder's more hateful than is sacrilege.
Thy actions ever have been honourable.
    Don Sago. And this the crown of all my actions,
To purge the earth of such a man turn'd monster.
    Rog. I never wrong'd thee, Spaniard; did I? speak;
I'll make thee satisfaction like a soldier,
A true Italian, and a gentleman.
Thy rage is treachery, without a cause.[70]
    Don Sago. My rage is just; and thy heart-blood shall know,
He that wrongs beauty must be honour's foe.
Isabel's quarrel arms the Spaniard's spirit.
    Rog. Murder should keep with baseness, not with merit.
I'll answer thee to morrow, by my soul,
And clear thy doubts, or satisfy thy will.
    Don Sago. He's war's best soldier, can with safety kill.
Take this to night;—*(Shoots him.)* now, meet with me to morrow.—
I come, Isabella; half thy hate is dead:
Valour makes murder light, which fear makes dread.

Enter the CAPTAIN *of the* GUARD, *with a band of Soldiers.*

    Captain. The pistol was shot here: seize him! Bring lights! What! Don Sago, Colonel of the horse! Ring the alarum-bell, raise the whole city! His troops are in the town; I fear treachery. Who's this lies murdered? Speak, blood-thirsty Spaniard!
    Don Sago. I have not spoil'd his face; you may know his visnomy.[71]
    Captain. 'Tis Count Rogero; go, convey him hence!—

---

[70] The 4tos. have here this unmeaning Stage-direction in the margin—*"Tell him all the Plot."*

[71] A corruption of physiognomy. It is used by Spenser.

Thy life, proud Spaniard, answers this offence.—
A strong guard for the prisoner, lest the city's power rise to rescue him!

[The Soldiers surround Don Sago.

    Don Sago. What needs this strife?
Know, slaves, I prize revenge above my life.
Fame's register to future times shall tell,
That by Don Sago, Count Rogero fell.

[Exeunt.

END OF ACT IV.

ACT V.

SCENE 1.—*Pavia.—The Castle Green—a Scaffold, &c.*

Enter DUKE *of* MEDINA.—*After him,* ROGERO'S *Body, borne by Attendants; then* DON SAGO, *guarded.* EXECUTIONER, *Soldiers, &c.*

Medina. Don Sago, quak'st thou not to behold this spectacle,
This innocent sacrifice, murder'd nobleness,
When blood, the Maker ever promiseth,
Shall, though with slow, yet with sure vengeance rest?
It is a guerdon earn'd, and must be paid;
As sure revenge, as it is sure a deed:
I ne'er knew murder yet, but it did bleed.
Can'st thou, after so many fearful conflicts
Between this object and thy guilty conscience,
(Now thou art freed from out the serpent's jaws,
That vile adulteress,[72] whose sorceries
Do draw chaste men into incontinence,
Whose tongue flows o'er with harmful eloquence,
Can'st thou, I say, repent this heinous act,
And learn to loathe that killing cockatrice?
   Don Sago. By this fresh[73] blood, that from thy manly breast
I cowardly struck out, I would in hell,
From this sad minute, till the day of doom,
To re-inspire vain Esculapius,
And fill these crimson conduits, feel the fire
Due to the damn'd, and to this horrid fact!
   Medina. Upon my soul, brave Spaniard, I believe thee!
   Don Sago. Oh! cease to weep in blood, or teach me too.

---

[72] *Adult'ress, Emp'ress,* &c. are merely contractions of *Adulteress, Emperess,* &c. as the words were anciently spelled.

[73] The 4to. reads "flesh-blood."

The bubbling wounds do murmur for revenge.
This is the end of lust, where men may see
Murder's the shadow of adultery,[74]
And follows it to death.

    Medina. But, hopeful lord, we do commiserate
Thy bewitch'd fortunes; and free pardon give,
On this thy true and noble penitence.
Withal, we make thee Colonel of our Horse,
Levied against the proud Venetian state.

    Don Sago. Medina, I thank thee not; give life to him
That sits with Risus and the full-cheek'd Bacchus,
The rich and mighty monarchs of the earth!
To me, life is ten times more terrible,
Than death can be to me. Oh! break, my breast!
Divines and dying men may talk of hell,
But, in my heart the several torments dwell.
What's Tanais, Nilus? or what's Tigris swift?
What Rhenus, fiercer than the Cataract?
Although Neptolis cold, the waves of all the Northern Sea,
Should flow for ever through these guilty hands,
Yet the sanguinolent stain would extant be.[75]

    Medina. God pardon thee! we do.

A shout.—Enter a MESSENGER.

    Messenger. The Countess comes, my lord, unto the death;
But, so unwillingly and unprepar'd,
That she is rather forc'd: thinking the sum,
She sent to you, of twenty thousand pounds,
Would have assur'd her life.

    Medina. O heavens!

---

[74] "Where whoredom reigns, there murder follows fast,
    "As falling leaves before the winter's blast."

R. Greene.

[75] Another imitation of Shakspeare. It is clear that the author had in his thoughts a passage in "Macbeth," Act II. Scene 2.

83

Is she not weary yet of lust and life?
Had it been Cræsus' wealth, she should have died.
Her goods, by law, are all confiscate to us;
And die she shall! Her lust
Would make a slaughter-house of Italy.
Ere she attained to four-and-twenty years,
Three Earls, one Viscount, and this valiant Spaniard,
Are known to ha' been the fuel to her lust;
Besides her secret lovers, which, charitably,
I judge to have been but few; but, some they were.
Here is a glass, wherein to view her soul;
A noble but unfortunate gentleman,
Cropp'd by her hand; as some rude passenger
Doth pluck the tender roses in the bud.
Murder and lust, the least of which is death;
And hath she yet any false hope of breath?

Enter the COUNTESS, *with her hair hanging down, a chaplet of flowers on
    her head, and a nosegay in her hand. Before her, an* EXECUTIONER; *and
    with her, a* CARDINAL.

    Countess. What place is this?
    Cardinal. Madam, the Castle-green.
    Countess. There should be dancing on a green, I think.
    Cardinal. To you, none other than your dance of death.
    Countess. Good, my Lord Cardinal, do not thunder thus;
I sent to day to my physician,
And, as he says, he finds no sign of death.
    Cardinal. Good madam, do not jest away your soul!
    Countess. (*To* Don Sago. O servant, how hast thou betray'd my life!
Thou art my dearest lover now I see;
Thou will not leave me till my very death.
Bless'd be thy hand! I sacrifice a kiss
To it and vengeance. Worthily thou did'st;
He died deservedly, not content t'enjoy
My youth and beauty, riches and my fortune;

But, like a chronicler of his own vice,
In epigrams and songs he tun'd my name;
Renown'd me for a strumpet, in the courts
Of the French King and the great Emperor.
Didst thou not kill him drunk?[76]

    Medina. O shameless woman!

    Countess. Thou should'st; or in th'embraces of his lust;
It might have been indeed a woman's vengeance.
Yet, I thank thee, and would not wish him living,
Were my life instant ransom'd.

    Cardinal. O madam, in your soul have charity.

    Countess. There's money for the poor.

[Gives him money.

    Cardinal. O lady, this is but a branch of charity,
An ostentation, or a lib'ral pride;
Let me instruct your soul, for that, I fear,
Within the painted sepulchre of flesh,
Lies in a dead consumption. Madam, read!

[Gives her a book.

    Countess. You put me to my book, my lord;
Will not that save me?

    Cardinal. Yes, madam, in the everlasting world.

    Sago. Amen! amen!

    Countess. While thou wert my servant, thou hast ever said
Amen to all my wishes: witness this spectacle.

[Pointing to Rogero's body.

Where's my Lord Medina?

    Medina. Here, Isabella; what would you?

    Countess. May we not be repriev'd?

    Medina. Mine honour's past, you may not.

    Countess. No, 'tis my honour's past.

    Medina. Thine honour's past, indeed!

    Countess. Then, there's no hope of absolute remission?

---

[76] The idea is borrowed from "Hamlet," Act Scene.

Medina. For that your holy confessor will tell you.
Be dead to this world! for, I swear you die,
Were you my father's daughter!
    Countess. Can you do nothing, my Lord Cardinal!
    Cardinal. More than the world, sweet lady; help to save
What hand of man wants power to destroy.
    Countess. You're all for this world; then, why not I?
Were you in health and youth, like me, my lord,
Although you merited the crown of life,
And stood in state of grace, assur'd of it;
Yet in this fearful separation,
Old as you are, e'en till your latest gasp
You'd crave the help of the physician;
And wish your days lengthen'd one summer longer.
Though all be grief, labour, and misery:
Yet none will part with it, that I can see.
    Medina. Up to the scaffold with her, it is late.
    Countess. Better late than never, my good lord.
You think you use square dealing, mighty duke,
Tyrant of France, sent hither by the devil.

[She ascends the scaffold.

    Medina. The fitter to meet you.
    Cardinal. Peace: good my lord, in death do not provoke her.
    Countess. Servant,

[To Don Sago.

Low as my destiny I kneel to thee,
Honouring in death, thy manly loyalty:
And whatsoe'er become of my poor soul,
The joys of both worlds evermore be thine.
Commend me to the noble Count Gniaca,
That should have shared thy valour, and my hatred.
Tell him I pray his pardon and forgiveness.
Medina, art thou yet inspir'd from heav'n,
Show thy Creator's image; be like him,
Father of mercy.

Medina. Head's-man, do thine office.

Countess. Now, God, lay all thy sins upon thy head,
And sink thee with them to infernal darkness,
Thou teacher of the Furies' cruelty.

Cardinal. O madam, teach yourself a better prayer,
This is your latest hour.

Countess. He is mine enemy; his sight torments me;
I shall not die in quiet.

Medina. I'll be gone: off with her head there.

                [*Exit.*

Countess. Tak'st thou delight, to torture misery?
Such mercy find thou in the day of doom.

Soldier. My lord, here is a holy friar desires.
To have some conference with the prisoners.

Enter ROBERTO, *in friar's weeds.*

Rob. It is in private what I have to say,
With favour of your fatherhood.

Cardinal. Friar, in God's name welcome.

         [Roberto *ascends to the Countess.*

Rob. Lady, it seems your eye is still the same,
Forgetful of what most it should behold:
Do not you know me then?

Countess. Most holy sir,
So far you are gone from my memory,
I must take truce with time, ere I can know you.

Rob. Bear record all you blessed saints in heav'n,
I come not to torment thee in thy death;
For of himself he's terrible enough:
But, call to mind a lady like yourself,
And think how ill in such a beauteous soul,
Upon the instant morrow of her nuptials,
Apostacy and wild revolt would shew:
Withal, imagine that she had a lord,

Jealous the air should ravish her chaste looks;[77]
Doating, like the Creator on his models,
Who views them every minute, and with care,
Mix'd in his fear of their obedience to him.
Suppose her sung through famous Italy,
More common than the looser songs of Petrarch,
To every several zany's instrument;
And he, poor wretch, hoping some better fate,
Might call her back from her adulterate purpose,
Lives in obscure, and almost unknown life;
Till, hearing that she is condemn'd to die,
For he once lov'd her, lends his pined corps,
Motion to bring him to her stage of honour,
Where drown'd in woe at her so dismal chance,
He clasps her,—thus he falls into a trance.[78]

    Countess. O my offended lord, lift up your eyes,
But yet avert them from my loathed sight.
Had I with you enjoyed the lawful pleasure,
To which belongs, nor fear, nor public shame,
I might have liv'd in honour, died in fame.
Your pardon on my fault'ring knees I beg,
Which shall confirm more peace unto my death,
Than all the grave instructions of the church.

    Rob. Pardon belongs unto my holy weeds;
Freely thou hast it: farewell, Isabella;
Let thy death ransom thy soul! Oh! die a rare example.
The kiss thou gav'st me in the church, here take;
As I leave thee, so thou the world forsake.

[Exit.

    Cardinal. Rare accident! ill welcome, noble lord:

---

    [77] "Hamlet" again:—

    "He might not beteem the airs of heav'n

    "Visit her face so roughly." Act Scene

    [78] Were it not for the *jingle*, I should feel convinced that this whole line is merely a Stage-Direction.

Madam, your executioner desires you to forgive him.

    Countess. Yes, and give him too: What must I do, my friend?

    Executioner. Madam, only tie up your hair.

    Countess. O these golden nets,

That have ensnar'd so many wanton youths,

Not one but has been held a thread of life,

And superstitiously depended on:—

Now to the block we must vail.[79] What else?

    Executioner. Madam, I must entreat you blind your eyes.

    Countess. I have lived too long in darkness, my friend;

And yet mine eyes, with their majestic light,

Have got new Muses in a poet's spright.[80]

They've been more gazed at than the God of Day;

Their brightness never could be flattered;

Yet thou command'st a fixed cloud of lawn,

T'eclipse eternally these minutes of light.

What else?

    Executioner. Now, madam, all's done,

And when you please I'll execute my office.

    Countess. We will be for thee straight.

Give me your blessing, my Lord Cardinal:

Lord, I am well prepar'd:

Murder and lust, down with my ashes sink,

But like ungrateful seed perish in earth,

That you may never spring against my soul,

Like weeds to choak it in the heavenly harvest!

I fall to rise, mount to thy Maker, spirit;

Leave here thy body, death has her demerit![81]

    Cardinal. A host of angels be thy convoy hence!

    Medina. To funeral with her body, and this lord's.

None here, I hope, can tax us of injustice;

---

[79] Vide Note 26.

[80] Vide Note 60.

[81] I imagine that our ancestors were here, by some contrivance, regaled with the spectacle of decapitation, as the original has this Stage-Direction—"Strike!"

She died deservedly, and may like fate
Attend all women so insatiate!   [*Exeunt.*

SCENE 2.—*Venice.*—*The Senate House.*

Enter DUKE AMAGO, *the* WATCH, *and Senators.*

Duke. I am amazed at this maze of wonder,
Wherein no thread or clue presents itself,
To wind us from the obscure passages.
What says my nephew?
　　Watch. Still resolute, my lord, and doth confess the theft.
　　Duke. We'll use him like a felon, cut him off,
For fear he do pollute our sounder parts.
Yet, why should he steal,
That is a loaden vine? riches to him,
Were adding sands unto the Lybian shore,
Or far less charity. What say the other prisoners?
　　Watch. Like men, my lord, fit for the other world;
They tak't upon their death, they slew your nephew.
　　Duke. And he is yet alive; keep them asunder;
We may scent out the wile.

Enter CLARIDIANA *and* MIZALDUS *bound, with a Friar and Officers.*

　　Miz. My friend, if 'tis the rigour of the law
I should be tied thus hard, I'll undergo it;
If not, then pr'ythee slacken; yet, I've deserv'd it;
This murder lieth heavy on my conscience.
　　Cla. Wedlock! Ay, here's my wedlock. O, whore! whore! whore!
　　Friar. O, Sir, be qualified.
　　Cla. Sir, I am to die a dog's death, and will snarl a little at the old Signor;
you are only a parenthesis, which I will leave out of my execrations. But first
to our quondam wives, that make us cry our vowels in red capital letters,—I.
and U. are cuckolds. Oh, may bastard-bearing, with the pangs of child-birth,
be doubled to them! may they have ever twins, and be three weeks in travail

between! may they be so rivelled with painting, by that time they are thirty, that it may be held a work of condign merit but to look upon 'em! may they live to ride in triumph in a dung-cart, and be crown'd with all the odious ceremonies belonging to't![82] may the cucking-stool[83] be their recreation, and a dungeon their dying chamber! may they have nine lives like a cat, to endure this, and more! may they be burnt for witches of a sudden! and lastly, may the opinion of philosophers prove true, that women have no souls!

Enter ABIGAIL *and* THAIS.

Abig. What, husband, at your prayers so seriously?

Cla. Yes, a few orisons. Friar, thou that stand'st between the souls of men and the devil, keep these female spirits away, or I will renounce my faith else.

Thais. Oh, husband! I little thought to see you in this taking.

Miz. Oh, whore! I little thought to see you in this taking. I am governor of this castle of cornets; my grave will be stumbled at, thou adulterate whore; I might have liv'd like a merchant.

Thais. So you may still, husband.

Miz. Peace! thou art very quick with me.

Thais. Ay, by my faith, and so I am, husband: belike, you know I am with child.

Miz. A bastard, a bastard, a bastard! I might have liv'd like a gentleman, and now I must die like a hanger-on. Shew tricks upon a wooden horse, and run through an alphabet of scurvy faces! Do not expect a good look from me.

Thais. Oh me, unfortunate!

Cla. Oh, to think, whilst we are singing the last hymn, and ready to be turned off, some new tune is inventing, by some metre-monger, to a scurvy ballad of our death![84] Again, at our funeral sermons, to have the divine divide

---

[82] This was formerly the common punishment of whores and bawds.

[83] Vide Note 23.

[84] So in Massinger's "Bondman:"—

> "*Timoleon.* What can'st thou say, to hinder
> "The course of justice?
>> "*Gracculo.* Nothing.—You may see
> "We are prepar'd for hanging, and confess
> "We have deserv'd it: our most humble suit is,

his text into fair branches! Oh, flesh and blood cannot endure it, yet I will take it patiently like a grave man.[85] Hangman, tie not my halter of a true lover's knot; I shall burst if thou dost.

Abig. Husband, I do beseech you on my knees, I may but speak with you. I'll win your pardon, or with tears like Niobe bedew a ——

Cla. Hold thy water, crocodile, and say I am bound to do thee no harm. Yet, were I free, I could not be looser than thou, for thou art a whore. Agamemnon's daughter, that was sacrific'd for a good wind, felt but a blast of the torments thou should'st endure; I'd make thee swoon oftener than that fellow, that by his continual practice hopes to become drum-major. What say'st thou to tickling to death with bodkins? but, thou hast laugh'd too much at me already, whore. Justice, O Duke, and let me not hang in suspence!

Abig. Husband, I'll nail me to the earth, but I'll win your pardon. My jewels, jointure, all I have, shall fly; apparel, bedding,—I'll not leave a rug, so you may come off fairly.

Cla. I'll come off fairly! Then beg my pardon! I had rather Chirurgions' Hall should beg my dead body for an anatomie, than thou beg my life. Justice, O Duke, and let us die!

Duke. Nay, Signor, think, and dally not with heaven,
But freely tell us, did you do the murther?

Miz. I have confest it to my ghostly father,
And done the sacrament of penance for it:
What would your highness more?

Cla. The like have I, what would your highness more?

"We may not twice he executed.
   "*Timoleon.* Twice! How mean'st thou?
   "*Gracculo.* At the gallows first, and after in a ballad
"Sung to some villanous tune. There are ten-groat rhymers
"About the town, grown fat on these occasions.
"Let but a chapel fall, or a street be fir'd,
"A foolish lover hang himself for pure love,
"Or any such like accident; and, before
"They are cold in their graves, some damn'd ditty's made,
"Which makes their ghosts walk."

[85] The author of this play has stolen even his quibbles from Shakspeare. *Mercutio* has in the present instance been land under contribution.

And here, before you all, tak't to my death.

    Duke. In God's name, then, on to the death with them.

For the poor widows that you leave behind,

Though by the law their goods are all confiscate,

Yet we'll be their good lord, and give 'em them.

    Cla. Oh, hell of hells! Why did not we hire some villain to fire our houses?

    Miz. I thought not of that, my mind was altogether of the gallows.

    Cla. May the wealth I leave behind me, help to damn her,

And at the cursed fate of courtezan,

What she gleans with her traded art,

May one, as a most due plague, cheat from her,

In the last dotage of her tired lust,

And leave her an unpitied age of woe.

    Miz. Amen, Amen.

    Watch. I never heard men pray more fervently.

    Miz. O that a man had the instinct of a lion, he knows when the lioness plays false to him; but these solaces, these women, they bring man to grey hairs before he be thirty; yet, they cast out such mists of flattery from their breath, that a man's lost again. Sure, I fell into my marriage-bed drunk, like the leopard; well, with sober eyes, would I had avoided it.

Come, grave, and hide me from my blasted fame;

O that thou could'st as well conceal my shame.

                [*Exeunt* Cla. *and* Miz. *with Officers.*

    Thais. Your pardon and your favour, gracious Duke,

                [Abig. & Thais *kneel to the* Duke.

At once we do implore, that have so long

Deceiv'd your royal expectation,

Assured that the comic knitting up

Will move your spleen unto the proper use

Of mirth, your natural inclination;

And wipe away the watery-colour'd anger,

From your enforced cheek. Fair Lord, beguile

Them and your servants with a pleasing smile.

    Duke. Now, by my life, I do; fair ladies, rise,

I ne'er did purpose any other end,

To them and these designs. I was inform'd,
Of some notorious error, as I sat in judgment; and, do you hear? these night-works require a cat's eyes to impierce dejected darkness. Call back the prisoners.

Re-enter CLARIDIANA *&* MIZALDUS, *with Officers.*

Cla. Now, what other troubled news, that we must back thus? Has any senator beg'd my pardon upon my wife's prostitution to him?

Miz. What a spite's this! I had kept in my breath of purpose, thinking to go away the quieter, and must we now back?

Duke. Since you're to die, we'll g1ve you winding—sheets,
Wherein you shall be shrouded while alive,
By which we wind out all these miseries.
Signor Mizaldus, bestow awhile your eye,
And read here of your true wife's chastity.

[*Gives him a Letter.*

Miz. Chastity! I will sooner expect a Jesuit's recantation, or the great Turk's conversion, than her chastity.
Pardon, my liege! I will not trust mine eyes:
Women and devils will deceive the wise.

Duke. The like, Sir, is apparent on your side.

[*To* Claridiana.

Cla. Who? my wife chaste? has your grace your sense? I'll. sooner believe a conjurer may say his prayers with zeal, than her honesty. Had she been an hermaphrodite, I would scarce have given credit to you.
Let him that hath drunk love-drugs, trust a woman;
By heaven, I think the air is not more common.

Duke. Then we impose a strict command upon you,
On your allegiance, read what there is writ.

Cla. A writ of error, on my life, my liege.

Duke. You'll find it so, I fear.

Cla. What have we here? the art of brachygraphy?

Thais. He's stung already, as if his eyes were turn'd on Perseus' shield.
Their motion's fixt, like to the pool of Styx.

Abig. Yonder's our flame, and from the hollow arches

94

Of his quick eyes, come comet trains of fire,
Bursting like hidden furies from their caves.

    Cla. (Reads.) "Your's, till he sleep the sleep of all the world,
"Mizaldus."

    Miz. Marry, an that lethargy seize you; read again.

    Cla. (*Reads again.*) "Thy servant, so made by his stars, Mizaldus."
A fire on your wand'ring stars, Mizaldus.

    Miz. Satan, why hast thou tempted my wife?

[To Cla.

    Cla. Peace, seducer! I am branded in the forehead with your star-mark.
May the stars drop upon thee, and with their sulphur vapours choak thee, ere
thou come at the gallows!

    Miz. Stretch not my patience, Mahomet.

    Cla. Termagant, that will stretch thy patience.

    Miz. Had I known this, I would have poison'd thee in the chalice this
morning, when we received the sacrament.

    Cla. Slave, know'st thou this? (*shews* Miz. *the ring.*) 'tis an appendix to the
letter; but, the greater temptation is hidden within. I will scour thy gorge like
a hawk; thou shalt swallow thine own stone in this letter,
"Seal'd and delivered in the presence of."

[They bustle.

    Duke. Keep them asunder! List to us, we command.

    Cla. O violent villain, is not thy hand hereto?
And writ in blood to shew thy raging lust?

    Thais. Spice of a new halter, when you go a ranging thus like devils, would
you might burn for't as they do.

    Miz. This 'tis to lie with another man's wife: he shall be sure to hear on't
again. But we are friends, sweet duke.
And this shall be my maxim all my life,
Man never happy is till in a wife.   [*Kisses* Thais.

    Cla. Here sink our hate lower than any whirlpool.
And this chaste kiss I give thee for thy care,
Thou fame of women, full as wise as fair.

[Kisses Abigail.

    Duke. You have saved us a labour in your love.

But, gentlemen, why stood you so prepost'rously?
Would you have headlong run to infamy,
In so defam'd a death?

    Miz. O my liege, I had rather roar to death with Phalaris' bull, than Darius like, to have one of my wings extend to Atlas, the other to Europe.

What's a cuckold learn of me,
Few can tell his pedigree,
Nor his subtle nature conster.
Born a man, but dies a monster.
Yet, great antiquaries say,
They spring from out Methuselah,
Who, after Noah's flood, was found
To have his crest with branches crown'd.
God, in Eden's happy shade,
This same wond'rous creature made.
Then, to cut off all mistaking,
Cuckolds are of women's making;
From whose snares, good Lord, deliver us.

    Cla. Amen! Amen! Before I would prove a cuckold, I would endure a winter's pilgrimage in the Frozen Zone, go stark-naked through Muscovia, where the climate is ninety degrees colder than ice. And thus much to all married men:—

Now I see great reason why
Love should marry jealousy:
Since man's best of life is fame,
He had need preserve the same;
When 'tis in a woman's keeping,
Let not Argus' eyes be sleeping.
The box unto Pandora given[86]
By the better powers of heaven,
(That contain'd pure chastity,
And each virgin sovereignty,)
Wantonly she op'd, and lost

---

[86] In the original, this line stands thus:—
        "The pox is unto panders given."

Gift whereof a god might boast.
Therefore, should'st thou Dian wed,
Yet be jealous of her bed.

    Duke. Night, like a mask, is enter'd heaven's great hall,[87]
With thousand torches ushering the way:
To Risus will we consecrate this evening;
Like Missermis cheating of the brach,[88]
We'll make this night the day. Fair joys befal
Us and our actions. Are you pleased all?

[Exeunt omnes.

FINIS.

---

[87] These two lines occur in a poem called "Myrrha, the Mother of Adonis," published in 1607 by W. BARKSTED, which circumstance strengthens the presumption that ho was the author of "The Insatiate Countess." It is indeed hardly possible to believe that Marston could have produced so despicable a composition, which I trust will never be allowed a place in any collection of his works.

[88] *i. e.* the bitch.

PRINCELYE PLEASURES
AT THE COURTE AT
KENELWOORTH

THAT IS TO SAYE,

The Copies of all such Verse, Proses, or Poeticall Inventions, and other
Deuices of pleasures, as were there deuised, and presented, by sundry
Gentlemen, before QVENE'S MAIESTIE,

IN THE YEARE

1575.

THE PRINTER TO THE READER

BEING advertised (gentle Reader) that in this last progresse, hir Maiestie (by the Ryght Noble Earle of Leycester) honorably and triumphantly receyved and entertained, at his Castle of Kenelwoorth: and that sundry pleasaunt and Poeticall inventions were there expressed, aswell in verse as in prose. All which have been sundrei tymes demaunded for, aswell at my handes, as also of other Printers, for that in deede, all studios and well disposed yong Gentlemen and others, were desyrous to be partakers of those pleasures by a profitable publication: I though meete to tyre by all meanes possible if I might recover the true Copies of the same, to gratifye all suche as had requyred them at my handes, or might hereafter bee styrred with the lyke desire. And in fine I have with much trauayle and paine obtained the very true and perfect Copies, of all that were there presented & executed: Ouer and besides, one Moral and gallant Deuyce, which neuer came to execution, although it were often in a readinesse. And these (being thus collected,) I have (for thy commoditie, gentle Reader,) now published: the rather because of a Report thereof lately imprinted by the name of the Pastime of the Progresse: which (in deede) doth nothing touche the particularitie of everye commendable action, but generally reherseth hir Maiesties cheereful entertainement in all places where shee passed: togither with the exceeding ioye that her subiects had to see hir: which Report made verye many desirous to have this perfect Copy: for that it plainlye doth set downe every thing as it was in deede presented, at large: And further doth declare, who was Aucthour and deviser of everye Poeme & invencion. So that I doubt not but it shall please & satisfye thee both with reason & contentacion: In full hope wherof, I leave thee to the reading of the same, & promise to be styl occupied in publishing such workes as may be both for thy pleasure and commoditie.

This 26. of March 1576.

A BRIEFE REHEARSALL, OR RATHER A TRUE COPIE, OF AS MUCH AS WAS PRESENTED BEFORE

HER MAJESTIE AT KENELWORTH,

DURING HER LAST ABOADE THERE, AS FOLLOWETH:

HER MAJESTY came thether (as I remember) on Saterday, being the nienth of July last past; on which day, there met her on the way, somewhat neere the Castle, *Sybilla*, who prophecied unto her Highness the prosperous raigne that she should continue, according to the happy beginning of the same. The order thereof was this: *Sybilla* being placed in an arbor in the parke, neere the highway where the *Queen's Majestie* came, did step out, and pronounced as foloweth:—

> All hayle, all hayle, thrice happy Prince; I am *Sibilla* she
> Of future chaunce and after happ, foreshewing what shall be.
> As now the dewe of heavenly gifts full thick on you doeth fall,
> Even so shall Vertue more and more augment your yeares withal.
> The rage of Warre, bound fast in chaines, shall never stirre ne move;
> But, Peace shall governe all your daies, encreasing subjects' love.
> You shal be called the Prince of peace, and peace shal be your shield,
> So that your eyes shall never see the broyls of bloody field.
> If perfect peace, then, glad your minde, he joyes above the rest,
> Which doth receive into his house so good and sweete a guest.
> And, one thing more I shall foretell, as by my skil I know,
> Your comming is rejoyced at, tenne thousand times, and mo.
> And, whiles your Highnes here abides, nothing shall rest unsought,
> That may bring pleasure to your mind, or quyet to your thought.
> And so, passe foorth in peace, O Prince, of high and worthy praise:
> The God that governes all in all, encrease your happy dayes!

This devise was invented, and the verses also written, by M. Hunneys, Master of her Majestie's Chappell.

Her Majesty passing on to the first gate, there stode, in the leades and battlements thereof, six trumpetters hugelie advaunced, much exceeding the common stature of men in this age, who had likewise huge and monstrous trumpettes counterfetted, wherein they seemed to sound; and behind them were placed certaine trumpetters, who sounded indeede at her Majestie's entrie. And by this dum shew it was ment, that in the daies and reign of King Arthure, men were of that stature; so that the Castle of Kenelworth should seeme still to be kept by Arthur's heires, and their servants. And when her Majestic entred the gate, there stood Hercules for Porter, who, seeming to be amazed at such a presence upon such a sodain, proffered to stay them. And yet, at last, being overcome by viewe of the rare beutie and princelie countenance of her Majestie, yeelded himselfe and his charge, presenting the keyes unto her Highnesse, with these words:—

> What stirre, what coyle is here? Come back! hold! whether now?
> Not one so stout to stir! what harrying have we here?
> My friends, a Porter I, no Poper here am plast:
> By leave, perhaps; els not, while club and limmes do last.
> A garboyle this, indeed! What yea, fair dames! what yea!
> What daintie darling's here? Oh God, a peerles Pearle!
> No worldly wight, no doubt; some soveraigne Goddes, sure!
> Even face, even hand, even eye, even other features all;
> Yea beutie, grace, and cheare, yea port and majestie,
> Shewe all, some heavenly peere, with vertues all beset.
> Come, come, most perfect Paragon, passe on with joy and blisse;
> Most worthy welcome Goddes guest, whose presence gladdeth all,
> Have here, have here, both club and keyes; myselfe, my warde I yielde;
> Even gates and all, yea Lord himselfe, submitte, and seeke your shielde.

These verses were devised and pronounced by; Master Badger, of Oxenforde, Maister of Arte, and Bedle in the same Universitie.

When her Majestie was entred the gate, and come into the base court, there came unto her a Ladie, attended with two Nimphes, who came all over the Poole, being so conveyed, that it seemed she had gone upon the water. This Ladie named herselfe the Ladie of the Lake, who spake to her Highnesse as followeth:—

> Though haste say On, let sute obtain some stay,
> (Most peerles Prince, the honour of your kinde,)

While that in short my state I doe display,
    And yeelde you thanks, for that which now I finde,
Who erst have wisht that death me hence had fet,
If Gods, not borne to die, had ought death any det.

I am the lady of this pleasant lake,
    Who, since the time of great King Arthure's reigne,
(That here with royal Court aboade did make,)
    Have led a lowring life, in restles paine;
Till now, that this your third arrival here,
Doth cause me come abroad, and boldly thus appeare.

For, after him, such stormes this Castle shooke,
    By swarming Saxons first, who scourgde this land,
As foorth of this my poole I nere durst looke,
    Though Kenelme, King of Merce, did take in hand
(As sorrowing to see it in deface)
To reare these ruines up, and fortifie this place.

For, straight, by Danes and Normans all this ile
    Was sore distrest, and conquered at last;
Whose force this Castle felt, and I therewhile
    Did hide my head; and though it straightway past
Unto Lord Sentloe's hands, I stode at bay,
And never shewed myself, but stil in keepe I lay.

The Earle Sir Moumford's force gave me no hart;
    Sir Edmund Crouchbacke's state, the Prince's sonne,
Could not cause me out of my lake to part;
    Nor Roger Mortimer's ruffe, (who first begun,
As Arthur's heir, to keepe the table round,)
Could not comfort my hart, or cause me come on ground.

Nor any owner els, not he that's now,
    (Such feare I felt again some force to feele,)
Tyl new the Gods doe seeme themselves t'allow
    My comming foorth, which at this time reveale,
By number due; that your thrice comming her
Doth bode thrise happy hope, and voides the place from feare.

> Wherefore, I wil attend while you lodge here,
> (Most peerles Queene) to Court to make resort;
> And as my love to Arthure dyd appeere,
> So shal't to you, in earnest and in sport.
> Passe on, Madame, you need no longer stand:
> The Lake, the Lodge, the Lord, are your's for to command.

These verses were devised and penned by M. Ferrers, sometime Lord of Misrule m the Court.

Her Majesty, proceeding towards the inner court, passed on a bridge, the which was rayled in on both sides. And on the toppes of the postes thereof were set sundrie presents, and giftes of provision: as wine, corne, fruites, fishes, fowles, instrements of musike, and weapons for martial defence. All which were expounded by an Actor clad like a Poet, who pronounced these verses in Latine:—

> Jupiter è summi dum vertice cernit Olympi,
> Hue Princeps Regina tuos te tendere gressus,
> Scilicet eximiæ succensus imagine formæ,
> Et memor antiqui qui semper ferverat ignis,
> Siccine Cælicolæ patientur turpiter (inquit)
> Muneris exortem reginam hoc visere castrum
> Quod tam lœta subit? Reliqui sensere Tonantis,
> Imperium Superi pro se dat quisque libenter.
> Musiculas Sylvanus aves, Pomonaque poma,
> Fruges alma Ceres, rorantia vina Lyæus,
> Neptunus pisces, tela et tutantia Mavors.
> Hœc (regina potens) Superi dant munera Divi;
> Ipse loci Dominus dat se Castrumque Kenelmi.

These verses were devised by Master Muncaster; and other verses, to the very self-same effect, were devised by M. Paten, and fixed over the gate in a frame. I am not very sure whether these, or Master Paten's, were pronounced by the Author, but they were all to one effect. This speech being ended, she was received into the inner court with sweet musicke. And so alighting from her horse, the drummes, fifes, and trumpets sounded; wherewith she mounted the stayres, and went to her lodging.

On the next day (being Sunday) there was nothing done until the evening, at which time there wer fire-works shewed upon the water, the which were both strange, and wel executed; as sometimes, passing under the water a long space, when all men had thought they had bene quenched, they would rise and mount out of the water again, and burne very furiously, untill they were utterlie consumed.

Now, to make some playner declaration and rehersall of all these things before her Majestie. On the x of Julie, there met her in the forest, as she came from hunting, one clad like a savage man, all in ivie, who, seeming to woonder at such a presence, fell to quarrelling with Jupiter, as followeth:—

O thund'ring Jupiter, which swayest the heavenly sword,
At whose command all Gods must crouch, and knowledge thee their Lord,
Since I (O wretch there whiles) am here by thy decree,
Ordeyned thus in savage wise for evermore to be;
Since, for some cause unknowen but only to thy wil,
I may not come in stately court, but feede in forrestes stilt,
Vouchsafe yet, greatest God, that I the cause may know,
Why all these worthy Lords and Peeres are here assembled so!
Thou knowest (O mighty God) no mind can be so base,
But needs must mount, if once it see a sparke of perfect grace;
And, since I see such sights, I mean such glorious dames,
As kindle might in frozen brestes a furnace full of flames,
I crave (great God) to know what all these Peers might be,
And what has moved these sundry shewes which I of late did see.
Enform me, some good man! speake, speake, some courteous. knight!
They all cry mumme; what shall I do? what sunne shall lend me light?
Well, Eccho, where art thou? Could I but Eccho finde,
Shee, would returne me answere yet, by blast of every winde.
Ho, *Eccho, Eccho*, ho! where art thou, *Eccho*, where?
Why, *Eccho* friend, where dwellest thou now? Thou woont'st to harbour here.

Eccho answered.

Eccho.   HERE!
Then tell thou me some newes;
For els my heart would burst with griefe; of trueth, it cannot choose.
Eccho.   CHOOSE!
Choose? Why But thou me helpe, I say my heart will breake;

And therefore, even of curtesie, I pray thee, *Eccho*, speake!
Eccho.   SPEAK!
I speak! yes, that I will, unlesse thou be too coye;
Then, tell me first, what is the cause that all the people joy?
Eccho.   JOY!
Joy? Surely that is so, as may full well be seene;
But, wherefore doe they so rejoice? Is it for King or Queene?
Eccho.   QUEENE!
Queene? What, the Queene of Heaven? They knewe her long agone!
No, sure, it is some Queene on earth, whose like was never none.
Eccho.   NONE!
O, then, it seemes the Queene of England for to be,
Whose graces make the gods to grudge; methinkes it should be shee.
Eccho.   SHEE!
And is it she indeede? Then, tell me what was ment
By every shew that yet was seen; good Eccho, be content.
Eccho.   CONTENT!
What meant the woman first, which met her as she came?
Could she devine of things to come, as Sibelles me the same?
Eccho.   THE SAME!
The same? What Sibill? she which useth not to lye?
Alas! what dyd that beldame there? What, dyd she prophecie?
Eccho.   PROPHECIE!
O, then, belike she causde the worthy Queene to knowe
What happy raigne she still should hold, since Heavens ordeyned so.
Eccho.   So!
And what ment those great men, which on the walles were seene?
They were some gyants, certainly; no men so bigge have been.
Eccho.   HAVE BEEN!
Have been? Why then they served King Arthur, man of might;
And ever since this Castle kept for Arthur's heyres by right?
Eccho.   RIGHT!
Well, Hercules stood bie; why came be from his dorter?
Or was it eke some monstrous man, appointed for a porter?
Eccho.   A PORTER!
A Porter? surely then, he eyther was accrased;
Or else, to see so many men, his spirits were amased.
Eccho.   AMASED!
Amased? So methought. Why did he let them passe,

And yield his keyes? Percase he knew his Master's will so was.
Eccho.   SO WAS!
Well then, dyd he but well; yet, sawe I yet a dame,
Much like the Lady of the Lake: perchaunce so was her name.
Eccho.   HER NAME!
Alas! and what could she (poor dame distrest) deserve?
I knewe her well: percase she came this worthy Queene to serve.
Eccho.   TO SERVE!
So would I her advise. But, what meant all those shifts
Of sundry things upon a bridge? Were these rewards or gifts?
Eccho.   GIFTS!
Gifts? What, sent from the gods, as presents from above?
Or pleasures of provision, as tokens of true love?
Eccho.   TRUE LOVE!
And, who gave all these gifts? I pray thee (*Eccho*) say?
Was it not he who (but of late) this building here did lay?
Eccho.   DUDLEY!
O, Dudley! so methought. He gave himself and all;
A worthy gift to be received, and so I trust it shall.
Eccho.   IT SHALL!
What meant the fierie flames, which through the waves so flue?
Can no colde answers quench desire? Is that experience true?
Eccho.   TRUE!
Well, *Eccho*, tell me yet, howe might I come to see
This comely Queene of whom we talke? Oh, were she now by thee!
Eccho.   BY THEE!
By me! Oh, were that true, how, might I see her face?
Howe might I knowe her from the rest, or judge her by her grace?
Eccho.   HER GRACE!
Well then, if so myne eyes be such as they have been,
Methinkes I see among them all, this same should be the Queene.
Eccho.   THE QUEENE!

Herewith, he fell on his knees, and spake as followeth:

O Queene, I must confesse, it is not without cause,
These civile people so rejoice that you should give them lawes!
Since I, which live at large, a wilde and savadge man,
And have ronne out a wilful race since first my lyfe began,

Do here submit myselfe, beseeching you to serve,
And that you take in worth, my will,—which can but well deserve.
Had I the learned skill which in your head is found,
My tale had flowed in eloquence, where nowe my words are drown'd.
Had I the bewtie's blase which shines in you so bright,
Then might I seeme a faulcon fayre, which nowe am but a kite.
Could I but touch the strings which you so heavenly handle,
I woulde confesse that Fortune then full freendly dyd me dandle.
O Queene without compare, you must not think it strange,
That here amid this wildernesss, your glorie so doth raunge;
The windes resound your worth, the rockes record your name,
These hills, these dales, these woods, these waves, these fields pronounce your
    fame;
And we which dwell abroade, can heare none other newes,
But tydings of an English Queene, whom Heaven hath dect with hewes.
Yea, since I first was borne, I never joyed so much,
As when I might behold your face, because I see none such.
And death, or drearie dole, (I knowe) will end my dayes,
As soon as you shall once depart, or wish to go your wayes.
But, comly peerlesse Prince, since my desires be great,
Walke here sometimes in pleasant shade, to fende the parching heat!
On Thursday next (thinke I) here will be pleasant dames,
Who bet then I may make you glee, with sundry gladsome games.
Meanwhile (good Queen) farewell; the gods your life prolong;
And take in worth the wilde man's words, for else you do him wrong.

Then he bad *Eccho* farewell, thus:

Eccho, likewise, farewell; let me go seeke some death;
Since I may see this Queene no more, good greefe nowe stop my breath!

These verses were devised, penned, and pronounced, by Master Gascoyne: and that (as I have heard credibly reported) upon a very great sudden.

The next thing that was presented before her Majestie, was the deliverie of the Lady of the Lake, whereof the sum was this:—Tryton, in likenesse of a Mermaide, came towarde the Queene's Majestie as she passed over the bridge, returning from hunting, and to her declared that Neptune had sent him to her Highnes, to declare the wofull distresse wherein the poore Ladie of the Lake did remaine; the cause whereof was this: *Sir Bruse, sauns pittié,* in revenge of his cosen Merlyne the Prophet, whom, for his inordinate lust, she had inclosed in a rocke, did continuallie pursue the Lady of the Lake, and had long sithens surprised her, but that Neptune, pitying her distresse, had envyroned her with waves; whereupon, she was enforced to live alwaies m that poole, and was thereby called the Lady of the Lake. Furthermore, affirming, that, by Merlyne's prophecie, it seemed she coulde never be delivered, but by the presence of a better maide than herselfe. Wherefore, Neptune had sent him, right humbly to beseech her Majestie, that she would no more but shew herselfe, and it should be sufficient to make Sir Bruse withdraw his forces. Furthermore, commanding both the waves to be calme, and the fishes to give their attendance. And this he expressed in verse, as followeth:—

The Speech of Tryton to the Queene's Majestie.

Muse not at all, most mightie Prince, though on this Lake you see
Me, Triton, floate, that in salt seas, among the gods, should be;
For, looke, what Neptune doth commaund, of Triton is obeyde,
And now in charge I am to guyde yon poore distressed mayde;
Who, when your Highnesse hither came, dyd humbly yeeld her lake,
And to attende upon your Court, did loyall promise make;
But, parting hence, that yrefull knight, Sir Bruce, had hyr in chase,
And sought by force her virgin's state full fowlie to deface.
Yea, yet at hand, about these bankes, his hands he often seene;
That neither can she come, nor scape, but by your helpe, O Queene.
For, though that Neptune has so fenst with floods her fortresse long,
Yet Mars her foe must needs prevaile, his batteries are so strong.
How then can Diane, Juno's force and sharpe assaults abyde,
When all the crue of cheefest gods is bent on Bruse his side?
Yea, oracle and propheizie say, ——sure she cannot stand,
Except a worthier maid than she her cause do take in hand.
Loe here, therefore, a worthy worke, most fit for you alone;
Her to defend and set at large (but you, O Queene,) can none;
And gods decree, and Neptune sues, this graunt, O peereles Prince;
Your presence onely shall suffice her enemies to convince.

Herewith, Triton sounded his trompe, and spake to the Winds, Waters, and Fishes, as followeth:—

You Windes, returne into your caves, and silent there remains;
You Waters wilde, suppresse your waves, and keepe you calme and plaine;
You Fishes all, and each thing else, that here have any sway,
I charge you all, in Neptune's name, you keepe you at a stay;
Until such time this puissant Prince, Sir Bruse hath put to flight,
And that the maide released be by soveraigne maiden's might!

This speach being ended, her Majestie proceeded further on the bridge, and the Ladie of the Lake (attended with her two Nimphes) came to her upon heapes of bulrushes, according to this former devise, and spake as followeth:—

> What worthy thankes might I, poore maide, expresse,
>   Or thinke in heart, that is not justly due
> To thee, (O Queene) which, in my great distres,
>   Succours hast sent, mine enemies to subdue?
> Not mine alone, but foe to ladyes all,
> That tyrant, *Bruce, sans pittié* whom we call.
>
> Untyll this day, the lake was never free
>   From his assaults, and other of his knights,
> Untill such tyme as he dyd playnely see
>   Thy presence dread, and feared of all wyghts;
> Which made him yeeld, and all his bragging bands:
> Resigning all into thy princely hands.
>
> For which great grace of liberty obtayned,
>   Not onely I, but Nymphs and Sisters all
> Of this large lake, with humble heart unfayned,
>   Render thee thankes, and honour thee withall;
> And, for playne proofe how much we do rejoyce,
> Expresse the same with tongue, with sound, and voice.

From thence, her Majestie passing yet further on the brydge, Protheus appeared, sitting on a dolphyn's back; and the dolphyn was conveyed upon a boate, so that the owers seemed to be his fynnes. Within the which dolphyn, a consort of musicke was secretly placed, the which sounded; and Protheus, clearing his voyce, sang this song of congratulation, as well m the behalfe of the Lady distressed, as also in the behalfe of all the Nimphs and Gods of the Sea:

The Song of Protheus.

O Noble Queene, give care to this my floating Muse,
And let the right of readie will my little skill excuse;
For, heardmen of the seas sing not the sweetest notes:
The winds and waves do roare and crie, where thus seldome floates.
Yet, since I doe my best, in thankfull wise to sing,
Vouchsafe (good Queene) that calm consent, these words to you may
    bring!
We yeeld you humble thanks, in mighthie Neptune's name,
Both for ourselves, and therewithall, for yonder seemly dame;
A dame, whom none but you deliver could from thrall;
Ne, none but you deliver us from loitring life withall.
She pined long in paine, as overworne with woes;
And we consumde in endless care, to fend her from her foes.
Both which you set at large, most like a faithful freend:
Your noble name be praisde therefore; and so my song I end!

This song being ended, Protheus told the Queene's Majestic a pleasant tale of his deliverie, and the fishes which he had in charge.

The devise of the Lady of the Lake, also, was Master Hunne's; and surely, if it had been executed according to the first invention, it had been a gallant shewe; for, it was first devised that, two dayes before the Ladie of the Lake's deliverie, a Captaine, with twentie or thyrtie shotte, shoulde have bene sent from the Hearon-house, (which represented the Lady of the Lake's Castell,) upon heapes of bulrushes; and, that Syr Bruse, shewing a great power upon the land, shoulde have sent out as many, or moe shot, to surprise the sayde Captayne; and so, they should have skirmished upon the waters, in such sort, that no man could perceive but that they went upon the waves. At last (Sir Bruse his men being put to flight) the Captaine should have come to her Majestie at the castell-window, and have declared more plainly the distresse of his Misstresse, and the cause that she came not to the Court, according to duetie and promise, to give hyr attendance; and that thereupon he should have besought hyr Majestie to succour his mistresse: the rather, because Merlin had

112

prophecied that she should never be delivered, but by the presence of a better maide than herselfe. This had not onely bene a more apt introduction to her deliverie, but also, the skirmish by night woulde have bene both very strange and gallant; and thereupon, her Majesty might have taken good occasion to have gone in her barge upon the water, for the better executing of her deliverie. The verses, as I thinke, were penned, some by Master Hunnes, some by Master Ferrers, and some by Master Goldingham.

And nowe, you have as much as I could recover hitherto of the devises executed there, the Coventrie shewe excepted, and the merry marriage, the which were so plaine, as needeth no further explication. To proceede, then, there was prepared a shew, to have bene presented before hyr Majestie in the Forest, the argument whereof was this:—

Dyana, passing in chase with her Nymphs, taketh knowledge of the countrie, and thereby calleth to minde how (neere seventeene yeares past) she lost in those coastes one of her best beloved Nimphes, called *Zabeta*. She describeth the rare vertues of *Zabeta*. One of her Nimphes confirmeth the remembrance thereof, and seemeth to doubt that dame *Juno* hath wonne *Zabeta* to be a follower of her's. Dyana confirmeth the suspition; but yet, affiying herselfe much in *Zabetae's* constancie, giveth charge to her Nimphes, that they diligently hearken and espie in all places, to finde or here newes of *Zabeta*; and so, passeth on.

To entertayne *intervallum temporis*, a man, cladde all in mosse, cometh in, lamentyng, and declaryng that he is the wylde man's sonne, which not long before, had presented hymselfe before hyr Majestie; and that his father, uppon such wordes as hyr Highnesse dyd then use unto him, lay languishing like a blind man, untill it might please hyr Highnesse to take the filme from his eyes.

The Nimphes returne, one after another, in quest of Zabeta; at last, Diana herself, returning, and hearing no newes of her, invoketh the helpe of her father, Jupiter. Mercurie commeth downe in a cloude, sent by Jupiter to recomfort Dyana, and bringeth her unto Zabeta. Diana rejoiceth, and after much friendly discourse, departeth, affiying herself in Zabetae's prudence and pollicie. She and Mercurie being departed, Iris commeth downe from the Rainebowe, sent by Juno, perswading the Queche's Majestie that she be not carried away with Mercurie's filed speeach, nor Dyanae's faire words; but, that she consider all things by proofe, and then she shall finde much greater cause to followe Juno than Dyana.

The Interlocutors were these:

Diana, Goddesse of Chastitie.
Castibula, Anamale, Nichalis, Diane's Nimphes.
Mercurie, Jove's Messenger.
Iris, Juno's Messenger.
Audax, the Soune of Silvester.

ACTUS I.   SCENA i.

Diana. Castibula.

Mine owne deere Nimphes, which knowledge me your Queene,
    And vow (like me) to live in chastitie,
My lovely Nimphes, which be as I have bene,
    Delightfull dames, and gemmes of jolytie;
Rejoysing yet much more to drive your dayes
    In life at large, that yeeldeth calme content,
Then wilfully to tread the wayward wayes
    Of wedded state, which is to thraldome bent;
I need not nowe, with curious speach, perswade
    Your chast consents in constant vowe to stande;
But yet, beware, least Cupid's Knights invade,
    By slight, by force, by mouth, or mightie hand,
The stately tower of your unspotted myndes!
    Beware (I say) least, whiles we walke these woods,
In pleasant chase of swiftest harts and hyndes,
    Some harmfull art entrap your harmlesse moodes.
You know, these holts, these hils, these covert places,
    May close convey some hidden force, unseene;
You see, likewise, the sundry gladsome graces,

Which in this soyle we joyfully have seene,
Are not unlike some Court to keepe at hand,
    Where guilefull tongues, with sweet, entising tales,
Might (Circes like) set all your ships on sand,
    And turne your present blysse to after bales.
In sweetest flowres, the subtyll snakes may lurke;
    The sugred baite oft hides the harmefull hookes;
The smoothest words draw wils to wicked worke;
    And deepe deceipts do follow fairest lookes.

Hereat pawsing, and looking about her, she tooke knowledge of the coast,
and proceeded.

But what, ahlas! oh, whyther wander wee?
    What chase hath led us thus into this coast?
By sundrie signes, I now perceive we be
    In Brutus' land, whereof he made such boast;
Which Albion, in olden days dyd hyght,
    And Brittaine next, by Brute his noble name;
Then Engiste's lande, as Chronicles do write;
    Now England, short, a land of worthy fame.
Ahlas, beholde, how memory breedes moone;
    Behold and see, how sight brings sorrow in;
My restless thoughts have made me woe-begon;
    My gasing eyes did all this grcef begin.
Beleeve me, (Nimphs) I feel great grips of greef,
    Which bruse my brest, to thinke, how here I lost
(Now long agoe) a love to me most lefe,
    Content you all, hyr whom I loved most.
You cannot chuse but call unto your mynde
    Zabetae's name, who twentie yeeres, or more,
Dyd follow me, still skorning Cupid's kinde,
    And vowing so to serve me evermore.
You cannot chuse but beare in memory
    Zabeta, hyr, whose excellence was such,
In all respects of every qualitie,

As gods themselves those gifts in her did grutch.
My sister first, which Pallas hath to name,
    Envyed Zabeta for hyr learned brayne;
My sister Venus feared Zabetae's fame,
    Whose gleames of grace hyr beutie's blase dyd stayne.
Apollo dread to touch an instrument,
    Where my Zabeta chaunst to come in place;
Yea, Mercuric was not so eloquent,
    Nor in his words had halfe so good a grace.
My stepdame, Juno, in hyr glyttering guyse,
    Was nothing like so heavenlie to beholde;
Short tale to make, Zabeta was the wight,
    On whom to thinke, my heart now waxeth cold.
The fearefull byrd oft lets hyr food, downe fall,
    Which findes her neast dispoyled of hyr yong;
Much like myselfe, whose minde such mones appale,
    To see this soyle, and therewithall among,
To thinke how, now neere seventeen yeeres agoe,
    By great myshap, I chaunst to leese her here;
But, my deere Nimphes, (on hunting as you go,)
    Looke narrowly, and hearken every where.
It cannot be, that such a starre as she
    Can leese her lyght for any lowring clowde;
It cannot be, that suche a saint to see,
    Can long inshrine her seemcly selfe so shroude.
I promise here, that she which first can bryng
    The joyful newes of my Zabetae's lyfe,
Shall never breake hyr bow, nor fret hyr string;
    I promise eke, that never storme of strife
Shall trouble hyr. Now, Nimphes, looke well about:
    Some happie eye spy my Zabeta out!

CASTIBULA.

O heavenly dame, thy wofull words have pearst
    The very depth of my forgetfull mynde;

And, by the tale which thou hast here rehearst,
    I yet record those heavenly gifts which shinde,
Triumphantly, in bright Zabetae's deedes.
    But, therewythall, a sparke of jellowsie,
With nice conceypt, my mynde thus farforth feedes,
    That she, which alwayes liked liberty,
And coulde not bowe to beare the servyle yoke
    Of false suspect, which mars these lovers' marts,
Was never wonne to lyke that smouldring smoke,
    Without some feate, that passeth common arts.
I dread, Dame Juno, with some gorgeous gift,
    Hath layde some snare, her fancie to entrap;
And hopeth so hyr loftie mynde to lyft
    On Hymen's bed, by height of worldly hap.

DIANA.

My loving Nimph, even so feare I likewise;
    And yet, to speake as truth and cause requires,
I never sawe Zabeta use the guyse,
    Which gave suspect of such unchast desires.
Full twenty yeeres I marked still hyr mynde,
    Ne could I see that any sparke of lust
A loytering lodge within her breast could finde.
    Howso it be, (deare Nimphes,) in you I trust,
To harke, and marke what might of hyr betyde,
    And what mishap withholds her thus from me.
High Jove himselfe my luckie steps so guyde,
    That I may once mine own Zabeta see!

Diana with her Nymphes proceede in chase; entertaine time, commeth in
one clad in mosse, as followeth:—

ACTUS I.   SCENA ii.

AUDAX solus.

If ever pitie pearst a peerlesse Princesse' breast,
Or ruthfull mone moved noble minde to graunt a just request,
Then, worthy Queene, give eare unto my woful tale,
For needes that sonne must sobbe and sigh, whose father bides in bale.
O Queene, O stately Queene, I am that wild man's sonne
Which, not long since, before you here presumed for to runne;
Who told you what he thought of all your vertues rare,
And therefore, ever since (and yet) he pines in woe and care.
Alas, alas, good Queene, it were a cruel deede,
To punish him which speakes no more but what he thinks indeede.
Especially when as all men with him consent,
And seeme with common voyce to prove the pith of his intent.
You heard what *Eccho* said to every word he spake;
You beare the speech of Dyanae's Nimphes, and what reports they make.
And can your highnesse then, condemne him to be blind?
Or can you so with needless greefe torment his harmless minde?
His eyes (good Queene) be great, so are they cleere and graye:
He never yet had pinne or webbe, his sight for to decay.
And sure, the dames that dwell in woods abroad with us,
Have thought his eyes of skil inough their beuties to discusse.
For proofe, your Majestie may now full plainly see,
He did not onely see you then, but more, he did foresee
What after should betide. He tolde you that (ere long)
You should finde here bright heavenly dames, would sing the selfe-same song.
And now you finde it true that he did then pronounce;
Your praises peyze by them a pound, which he weyed but an ounce.
For sure he is nor blinde, nor lame of any limme;
But yet, because you told him so, he doubts his eyes are dimme.
And I therefore (his sonne) your highnesse here beseech
To take in worth (as subject's due) my father's simple speech.
And if you finde some filme that seemes to hide his eyes,

118

Vouchsafe (good Queene) to take it off, in gratious woonted wise.
He sighing lies, and saies, "God put mine eyes out cleane:
"Ere choice of change in England fall to see another Queen!"

FINIS—*Actus 1.*

ACTUS II.   SCENA i.

ANAMALE sola.

Would God, I either had some Argus' eyes,
    Or such an ear as every tydings heares!
Oh, that I could some subtiltie devise,
    To heare or see what moulde Zabeta beares!
That so, the moode of my Dyanae's minde
    Might rest (by me), contented or appeased;
And I likewise might so her favour finde,
    Whom (Goddess like) I wish to have wel pleased.
Some courteous winde, come, blowe me happy newes;
    Some sweete birde, sing, and shewe me where she is;
Some Forrest God, or some of Faunus' crues,
    Direct my feete, if so they tread amisse!

ACTUS II.   SCENA ii.

NICHALIS sola.

If ever *Eccho* sounded at request,
    To satisfie an uncontented mind,
Then, *Eccho*, now come helpe me in my quest,
    And tel me where I might Zabeta find!
Speake, *Eccho*, speake! where dwels Zabeta, where?
    Alas, alas, or she, or I am deafe!
She answereth not. Ha! what is that I heare?
    Alas, it was the shaking of some leafe!

Wel, since I heare not tidings in this place,
    I will goe seeke her oute in some place els;
And yet, my mind divineth in this case,
    That she is here, or not farre off she dwels.

ACTUS II.   SCENA iii.

DIANA with her Traine.

No newes, my Nimphes? Wel, then, I may well thinke
    That carelessly you have of her enquired;
And, since from me in this distresse you shrinke,
    While I meanewhile my wearie limmes have tyred,
My father, Jove, vouchsafe to rue my greefe,
    Since here on earth I call for helpe in vaine!
O king of kings, send thou me some releefe,
    That I may see Zabeta once againe!

ACTUS II.   SCENA iv.

MERCURY, DIANA, and the Nimphes.

O Goddes, ceasse thy mone; thy plaints have pearst the skies;
And Jove, thy frendly father, hath vouchsaft to heare thy cries:
Yea more, he hath vouchsalt, in hast, post hast, to send
Me downe from heaven, to heale thy harme, and all thy misse to mend.
Zabeta, whom thou seekest, in heart, even yet, is thine;
And passinglie, in woonted wise, her vertues still doe shine.
But, as thou doest suspect, Dame Juno trained a trap,
And, many a day, to winne her wil, hath lulde her in her lap.
For first, these sixteene yeres, she hath beene daily seene,
In richest realme that Europe hath, a comlie crowned Queene.
And Juno hath, likewise, suborned sundric kings,
The richest and the bravest both that this our age foorth brings,

With other worthy wights, which sue to her for grace,
And, cunningly, with queint conceits doe pleade the lover's case.
Dame Juno geves her wealth, Dame Juno geves her case,
Dame Juno gets her every good that woman's wil may please.
And so, in joy and peace, she holdeth happy daies;
Not as thou thought'st; nor done to death, or woonne to wicked wayes.
For, though she finde the skil a kingdome for to weelde,
Yet cannot Juno winne her will, nor make her once to yeelde
Unto the wedded life; but, still she lives at large,
And holdes her neck from any yoke, without controll of charge.
Thus much it pleased Jove that I to thee should say;
And furthermore, by words exprest, he bade I should not stay;
But, bring thee to the place wherein Zabeta bides,
To prop up so thy stag'ring mind, which in these sorrowes slides.
O Goddes, then, he blithe; let comfort chase out greef;
Thy heavenly father's will it is to lend thee such releef.

DIANA.

O noble Mercurie, doest thou me then assure
That I shall see Zabetae's face; and that she doeth endure,
Even yet, in constant vowe of chaste unspotted life;
And that my stepdame cannot yet make her a wedded wife?
If that be so indeede, O Muses, helpe my voice,
Whom greefe and grones have made so hoarce, I cannot wel rejoyce!
O Muses, sound the praise of Jove his mighty name;
And you, deere Nimphes, which me attend, by duetie doe the, same!

Here Dyana, with her Nimphes, assisted by a consort of musicke unseene, shoulde sing this song, or rondled, following:—

O Muses, now come helpe me to rejoice,
    Since Jove hath changed my greefe to sodain joy;
And since the chaunce whereof I craved choice
    Is graunted me, to comfort mine annoy;
O, praise the name of Jove, who promist plaine

That I shall see Zabeta once againe!

O Gods of woods, and Goddes Flora eke,
    Now cleare your brestes, and beare a part with me;
My jewel she, for whom I woont to seeke,
    Is yet full safe, and soone I shall her see.
O, praise the name of Jove, who promist plaine
That I shall see Zabeta once againe!

And you, deere Nimphes, who know what cruel care
    I bare in brest, since she from me did part,
May wel conceive what pleasures I prepare,
    And how great joyes I harbour in my hart.
Then, praise the name of Jove, who promist plaine
That I shall see Zabeta once againe!

MERCURIE.

Come, Goddes, come with me; thy leysures last too long;
For, now thou shalt her here beholde for whom thou sing'st this song.
Behold, where here she sits, whom thou so long hast sought!
Embrace her, since she is to thee a jewel dearly bought!
And I wil now returne to God in heaven on hie,
Who graunt you both always to please his heavenly majestie!

Mercury departeth to heaven.

[DIANA.]

What, doe I dreame, or doth my minde but muse?
    Is this my leefe, my love, and my delight?
Or, dyd this God my longing minde abuse,
    To feede my fancie with a fained sight?
Is this Zabeta? Is it she indeede?
    It is she sure! Zabeta mine, all haile!
And, though Dame Fortune seemeth you to feede

With princely port, which serves for your availe,
Yet, geve me leave to gaze you in the face,
    Since (now long since) myselfe yourselfe did seeke;
And be content, for all your statelie grace,
    Stil to remaine a maiden alwaies meeke.
Zabeta mine, (now Queene of high renowne,)
    You know how wel I loved you alwaies;
And, long before you did atcheeve this crowne,
    You knowe how wel you seemde to like my wayes.
Since when, you (woon by Juno's gorgeous giftes)
    Have left my lawndes, and closely kept in Court;
Since when, delight, and pleasure's gallant shifts,
    Have fed your minde with many a princely sport.
But, peereles Queene, (sometime my peereles maide,
    And yet, the same, as Mercurie doeth tel,)
Had you but knowen how much I was dismaide,
    When first you did forsake with me to dwel,—
Had you but felt what privie panges I had,
    Because I could not finde you foorth againe,
I know full wel, yourselfe would have beene sad,
    To put me so to proofe of pinching paine.
Well, since Dan Jove (my father) me assures
    That, notwithstanding all my stepdame's wyles,
Your maiden's minde yet constant stil endures,
    Though wel content a Queene to be therewiles,—
And since, by prudence and by pollicie,
    You winne from Juno so much worldly wealth,
And since the piller of your chastitie
    Still standeth fast, as Mercurie me telleth,
I joy with you, and leave it to your choice
    What kinde of life you best shall like to holde;
And, in meane while, I cannot but rejoyce,
    To see you thus bedect with glistering golde;
To see you have this traine of stately dames,
    Of whom, eche one may seeme some Goddes' peere;

And you yourselfe (by due desert of fame)
  A Goddes full; and so, I leave you here.
It shall suffice, that on your faith I trust;
  It shall snuffice, that once I have you seene;
Farewell! not as I would, but as I must:
  Farewel, my Nimphe! Farewel, my noble Queen!

Diana, with her Traine, departeth.

ACTUS II.   SCENA VLTIMA.

IRIS sola.

Oh, loe, I come to late! Oh, why had I no wings?
To helpe my willing feste, which fet these hastie frisking flings?
Ahlas, I come too late! that babling God is gone;
And Dame Diana fled likewise: here standes the Queene alone.
Well, since a booteles plaint but little would prevaile,
I will goe tell the Queene my tale. O peereles Prince, all haile!
The Queene of Heaven herselfe did send me, to controle
That tatling traytor Mercurie, who hopes to get the gole
By curious filed speech, abusing you by arte;
But, Queene, had I come scone inough, he should have felt the smart.
And you, whose wit excelles, whose judgement hath no peere,
Beare not in minde those flattering words which he expressed here!
You know that in his tongue consistes his cheefest might;
You know his eloquence can serve to make the crowe seem white;
But, come to deedes, indeede, and then you shall perceive
Which Goddes meanes your greatest good, and which would you deceive.
Call you to minde the time, in which you did insue
Dianae's chase, and were not yet a guest of Juno's crue;
Remember all year life before you were a Queene,
And then compare it with the daies which you since then have seene.
Were you not captive caught? Were you not kept in walles?
Were you not forst to leade a life like other wretched thralles?

Where was Diana then? Why did she you not ayde?
Why did she not defend your state, which were and are her maide?
Who brought you out of bryers? Who gave you rule of realmes?
Who crowned first your comely head with princely dyademes?
Even Juno, she which meant, and yet doeth meane, likewise,
To geve you more than will can wish, or wit can wel devise.
Wherefore, good Queene, forget Dianae's tysing tale;
Let never needlesse dread presume to bring your blisse to bale!
How necessarie 'twere for worthy Queenes to wed,
That know you wel, whose life always in learning hath beene led.
The countrey craves consent; your vertues vaunt themselfe;
And Jove in heaven would smile to see Diana set on shelfe.
His Queene hath sworne (but you) there shal no me be such:
You know she lies with Jove a' nights, and night ravens may doe much.
Then, geve consent, O Queene, to Juno's just desire;
Who, for your wealth, would have you wed; and, for your farther hire,
Some Empresse wil you make; she had me tel you thus:—
Forgave me, Queene, the words are her's; I come not to discusse;
I am but messenger; but, sure, she bade me say,
That where you now in princely port have past one pleasant day,
A world of wealth at wil you hencefoorth shall enjoy,
In wedded state; and therewithall holde up from great annoy
The staffe of your estate. O Queene, O worthy Queene,
Yet never wight felt perfect blis, but such as wedded beene!

Tam Marti, quam Mercurio.

This shewe was devised and penned by M. Gascoigne; and, being prepared and redy (every actor in his garment) two or three dayes together, yet never came to execution. The cause whereof I cannot attribute to any other thing, than to lack of opportunitie and seasonable weather.

The Queene's Majestie hasting her departure from thence; the Earle commanded Master Gascoigne to devise some Farewel, worth the presenting. Whereupon, he himselfe clad like unto Sylvanus, God of the Woods, and meeting her as she went on hunting, spake, *ex tempore*, as followeth:—

Right excellent puyssant, and most happy Princesse, whiles I walke in these woodes and wildernes, (whereof I have the charge,) I have often mused with myselfe, that your Majesty, being so highly esteemed, so entirely beloved, and so largely endued by the Celestial powers, you can yet continually give eare to the councel of these terrestrial companions, and so consequently passe your time wheresoever they devise or determine that it is meete for your royal person to be resident. Surely, if your Highnesse did understand (as it is not to me unknowen) what pleasures have been for you prepared, what great good-will declared, what joy and comfort conceived in your presence, and what sorowe and greefe sustained by likelihode of your absence, (yea, and that by the whole bench in Heaven,) since you first arryved in these coastes, I thinke it would be sufficient to drawe your resolute determination for ever to abide in this countrey, and never to wander any further by the direction and advice of these peers and councellers; since thereby the heavens might greatly be pleased, and most men throughly recomforted. But, because I rather wish the increase of your delights, then any way to diminish the heape of your contentment, I will not presume to stay your hunting, for the hearing of my needelesse, thriftlesse, and bootelesse discours; but, I doe humbly beseech that your Excellencie will geeve me leave to attend you, as one of your footemen, wherein I undertake to doe you double service; for, I will not only conduct your Majestie in safetie from the perillous passages which are in these woods and forrests, but will also recount unto you (if your Majestie vouchsafe to hearken thereunto) certaine adventures, neither unpleasant to heare, nor unprofitable to be marked.

Herewith, her Majestie proceeded, and Sylvanus continued as followeth:—

There are not yet twenty daies past (most noble Queene) since I have beene, by the Procuror-generale, twise severally summoned to appeare before the great Gods in their councel-chamber; and, making mine appearance, according to my duety, I have seene in heaven two such exceedyng great contraryetyes, or rather two such woonderfull changes, as drawe me into deepe admiration and suddayne perplexitie. At my first comming, I found the whole company of heaven in such a jollitie, as I rather want skill to expresse it lively, then wil to declare it redily. There was nothing in any corner to be seene but rejoysing and mirth, singing, daunsing, melody and harmony, amiable regardes, plentiful re wards, tokens of love and great good-wil, tropheys and triumphes, gifts and presents:—alas, my breath and memorie faile me!—leaping, frisking, and clapping of hands.

To conclude, there was the greatest feast and joye that ever eye sawe, or eare heard tell of, since heaven was heaven, and the earth began to have his being. And, enquiring the cause thereof, *Reason*, one of the heavenly ushers, tolde me that it was to congratulate for the comming of your most excellent Majestie into this countrey. In very deede, to confesse a trueth, I might have perceived no les by sundry manifest tokens here on earth; for, even here, in my charge, I might see the trees florish in more than ordinarie bravery, the grasse growe greener than it was woont to doe, and the deere went tripping (though against their death) in extreme delicacie and delight. Wel, to speake of that I sawe in heaven,—every God and Goddes made all preparations possible to present your Majestie with some acceptable gift; thereby to declare the exceeding joy which they conceived in your presence. And I, poor Rurall God, which am but seldome called amongst them, and then, also, but slenderly countenanced, yet, for my great good-will towardes your Majestie, no way inferior to the proudest God of them all, came downe againe with a flea in mine eare, and began to beate my braines for some device of some present, which might both bewray the depth of mine affections, and also be worthy for so excellent a Princesse to receive. But, whiles I went so musing with myselfe, many, yea too many, dayes, I found by due experience, that this proverbe was all too true, *Omnis mora trahit periculum*. For, whiles I studied to atcheeve the height of my desires, beholde, I was the second time summoned to appeare in heaven. What sayd I, heaven? No, no, most comely Queene; for, when I came there, heaven was not heaven; it was rather a verye hell. There was nothing but weeping and wayling, crying and howling, dole, desperation, mourning, and moane. All which I perceived also here on earth, before I went up; for, of a trueth (most noble Princesse) not only the skies scowled, the windes raged, the waves rored and tossed; but also the fishes in the waters turned up their bellies, the deere in the woods went drowping, the grasse was wery of growing, the trees shooke off their leaves, and all the beastes of the forrest stoode amazed. The which sudden change, I plainly perceyved to be for that they understood above, that your Majestie would shortly (and too speedely) depart out of this countrey, wherein the heavens have happely placed you, and the whole earth earnestly desireth to keepe you. Surely (gracious Queene) I suppose that this late alteration in the skyes hath seemed unto your judgement droppes of raine in accustomed maner. But, if your Highnesse will beleeve me, it was nothing els but the very flowing teares of the Gods, who melted into moane for your hastie departure.

Well, because we Rurall Gods are bound patiently to abide the censure of the Celestiall bench, I thought meete to hearken what they would determine; and, for a finall conclusion, it was generally determined that some convenient messenger should be dispatched with all expedition possyble, as wel to beseech your Majestie that you would here remaine, as also further to present you with the proffer of any such commodities and delights, as might draw your full consent to continue here, for their contentation, and the generall comfort of men.

Here her Majestie stayed her horse, to favour Sylvanus, fearing least he should be driven out of breath, by following her horse so fast. But, Sylvanus humbly besought her Highnesse to goe on; declaring that if hys rude speech did not offend her, he coulde continue this tale to be twenty miles long. And therewithall protested that hee had rather be her Majestie's footeman on earth, then a God on horseback in heaven; proceeding as followeth:

Now, to returne to my purpose, (most excelent Queene,) When I had heard their deliberation, and called unto minde that sundry realmes and provinces had come to utter subvertion by over-great trust given to ambassadors, I (being thorowly tickled with a restlesse desire) thought good to pleade in person; for, I will tell your Majestie one strange propertie that I have: there are fewe, or none, which know my minde so well as myselfe; neither are there many which can tel mine owne tale better than I myselfe can do. And therefore I have continually awayted these 3 dayes, to espie when your Majestie would (in accustomed manner) come on hunting this way. And being now arrived most happely into the porte of my desires, I wil presume to beseech most humbly, and to intreate most earnestly, that your Highnes have good regard to the general desire of the Gods, together with the humble petitions of your most loyal and deeply affectionate servants.

And, for my poore part, in full token of my duetiful meaning, I here present you the store of my charge, undertaking that the deare shal be dayly doubled, for your delight in chase. Furthermore, I will intreate Dame Flora to make it continually Spring here, with store of redolent and fragrant flowers. Ceres shall be compelled to yeelde your Majestie competent provision; and Bacchus shal be sued unto, for the first-fruits of his vineyards. To be short, O peerelesse Princes, you shall have all things that may possibly be gotten for the furtheraunce of your delights. And I shall be most glad and triumphant, if I may place my Godhead in your service perpetually. This tedious tale, O comely Queene, I began with a bashfull boldnes; I have continued in base eloquence; and I cannot better knit it up, then, with homely humilitie, referring the consideration of these my simple wordes unto the deepe discretion of your princelie will. And now, I wil, by your Majestie's leave, turne my discourse into the rehearsal of strange and pitifull adventures.

So it is, good gracious lady, that Diana passeth oftentimes through this forest, with a stately traine of gallant and beutifull Nimphes; amongst whome, there is one surpassing all the rest for singuler gifts and graces; some call her *Zabeta*; some other have named hyr *Ahtebasile,* some *Completa,* and some *Complacida:* whatsoever hyr name be, I will not stande upon it. But, as I have sayde, her rare giftes have drawne the most noble and worthy personages in the whole world to sue unto hyr for grace; all which she hath so rigorously repulsed, or rather (to speake playne English) so obstinately and cruelly rejected, that I sigh to thinke of some their mishaps. I allowe and commende her justice towardes some others; and yet, the teares stande in mine eyes, yea, and my tongue trembleth and faltereth in my mouth, when I begin to declare the distresses wherein some of them doe presently remayne. I could tell your Highnesse of sundry famous and worthy persons, whome shee hath turned and converted into most monstrous shapes and proportions: as, some into fishes, some other into foules, and some into huge stony rocks and great mountaines; but, because diverse of hyr most earnest and faithfull followers, as also some cicophants, have been converted into sundry of these plants whereof I have charge, I will on shew unto your Mjestiea so many of them as are in sight in these places where you passe.

Behold, gratious Lady, this old Oke. The same was many yeeres a faithfull follower and trustie servant of hyr's, named *Constance;* whome, when shee coulde by none other meanes overthrowe, considering that no chaunge coulde creepe into his thoughtes, nor any trouble of passions and perplexities coulde turne his resolute minde, at length she caused him, as I say, to be converted into this Oke: a strange and cruell metamorphosis. But yet, the heavens have thus far forth favoured and rewarded his long-continued service, that as in life he was unmovable, even so now all the vehement blasts of the most raging windes cannot once move his rocky body from his rooted place and abyding. But, to countervaile this cruelty with a shewe of justice, she converted his contrarie, *Inconstancie,* into yonder Popler, whose leaves move and shake with the least breath or blast.

As also, shee dressed *Vaineglory* in his right coulours, converting him into this Ash-tree; which is the first of my plants that buddeth, and the first likewise that casteth leafe. For, beleeve me, most excellent Princesse, *Vaineglory* may well begin hastily, but seldome continueth long.

Againe, she hath well requited that busie elfe, *Contention*, whom she turned into this Bramble-Bryer, the which, as your Majestie may well see, dooth even yet catch and snatch at your garments, and every other thing that passeth by it. And, as for that wicked wretch, *Ambition*, she dyd, by good right, condemne hym into this braunch of Ivy, the which can never clyme on hygh, nor florysh, without the helpe of some other plant or tree; and yet, commonly, what tree soever it ryse by, it never leaveth to wynde about it, and strayghtly to infolde it, untyll it have smowldred and killed it. And, by your leave, good Queene, such is the unthankfull nature of cankred ambitious myndes, that commonly they maligne them by whom they have rysen, and never cease, untyll they have brought them to confusion. Well, notwithstanding these examples of justice, I will nowe rehearse unto your Majestie such a straunge and cruell metamorphosis, as, I think, must needes move your noble minde unto compassion. There were two sworne brethren, which long time served hyr, called *Deepedesire* and *Denedesert*; and, although it bee very hard to part these two in sunder, yet it is sayd that she dyd, long sithens, convert *Duedesert* into yonder same Lawrell-tree. The which may very well be so, consideryng the etimologie of his name; for, we see that the Lawrelle-braunch is a token of triumph in all trophies, and given as a reward to all victors: a dignitie for all degrees; consecrated and dedicate to Apollo and the Muses, as a worthie flower, leafe, or braunch, for their due deserts. Of him I will hold no longer discourse, because hee was metamorphosed before my tyme; for, your Majestie must understand that I have not long helde this charge, neyther do I meane long to continue in it; but, rather, most gladly to followe your Highnesse wheresoever you shall be come.

But, to speake of *Deepedesire*, that wretch of worthies, and yet the worthiest that ever was condemned to wretched estate. He was such an one, as neither any delay could daunt him, no disgrace could abate his passions, no tyme coulde tyre him, no water quench his flames, nor death itself could amase him with terror; and yet, this straunge starre, this courteous cruell, and yet the cruellest courteous that ever was; this *Ahtebasile, Zabeta*, or by what name soever it shall please your Majestie to remember hyr, did never cease to use imprecation, invocation, conjuration, and all meanes possible, untill she had caused him to be turned into this Holy-bush; and, as he was in this life and worlde continually full of compunctions, so is he now furnished on every side with sharpe pricking leaves, to prove the restlesse prickes of his privie thoughts. Mary, there are two kinds of Holly, that is to say, He-Holly and She-

Holly. Nowe, some will say, that the She-Holly hath no prickes: but, thereof I entermeddle not.

At these wordes: her Majestie came by a close arbor, made all of hollie; and whiles Silvanus pointed to the same, the principall bush shaked. For therein were placed, both straunge musicke, and one who was there appointed to represent *Deepedesire*. Silvanus, perceiving the bush to shake, continued thus:

Beholde, most gratious Qucene, this Holly-bush doeth tremble at your presence; and therefore I beleeve that *Deepedesire* hath gotten leave of the Gods to speake unto your excellent Majestie in their behalfe; for, I myselfe was present in the councell-chamber of Heaven, when *Desire* was thought a meete messenger to be sent from that convocation, unto your Majestie, as ambassadour; and, give eare good Queene: methinkes I hear his voyce.

Herewith, *Deepedesire* spake out of the Holly-bush, as followeth:

Stay, stay your hastie steppes, O Queene without compare,
And heare him talke, whose trusty tongue consumed is with care!
I am that wretch, *Desire*, whom neither death could daunt,
Nor dole decay, nor dread delay, nor fayned cheere inchant;
Whom neither care could quench, nor fancie force to change;
And therefore turned into this tree; which sight, percase, seems
    strange.
But, when the Gods of Heaven, and Goddesses withall,
Both Gods of Fieldes, and Forrest Gods, yea, Satires, Nimphes, and
    all,
Determined a dole, by course of free consent,
With wailing words, and mourning notes, your partyng to lament,
Then thought they meet to chuse me, silly wretch, *Desire*,
To tell a tale that might bewray as much as they requyre.
And hence, proceedes, O Queene, that, from this Holly-tree,
Your learned cares may heare him speake, whom yet you cannot see.
But, Queene, beleeve me nowe, although I do not sweare,
Was never greefe, as I could gesse, which sat their harts so neere,
As when they heard the newes that you, O royall Queene,
Would part from hence; and, that to proove, it may full well be scene.

For, marke what teares they shed these five dayes past and gone:
It was no rayne of honestie, it was great floods of mone.
As, first Diana wept such brynish bitter teares,
That all hyr Nimphes dyd doubt hyr death: hyr face the signe yet
    beares.
Dame Flora fell on ground, and brusde hyr wofull breast:
Yea, Pan dyd breake his oten pipes: Sylvanus, and the rest,
Which walke amid these woods, for greefe did rore and cry:
And Jove, to shew what mone he made, with thundring crackt the
    skye.
O Queene, O worthy Queene, within these holts and hilles,
Were never heard such greevous grones, nor seene such wofull wils!
But, since they have decreed, that I, poore wretch, *Desire*,
In their behalfe, shall make their mone, and comfort thus require,
Vouchsafe, O comely Queene, yet longer to remayne,
Or still to dwell amongst us here! O Queene, commaund againe
This Castle, and the Knight which keepes the same for you;
These woods, these waves, these fouls, these fishes, these deere, which
    are your dew!
Live here, good Queene, live here! you are amongst your friends;
Their comfort comes when you approch; and, when you part, it ends.
What fruits this soyle may serve, thereof you may be sure:
Dame Ceres and Dame Flora both will with you still indure.
Diana would be glad to meet you in the chase;
Silvanus, and the Forrest Gods, would follow you apace.
Yea, Pan would pipe his part, such daunces as he can;
Or els, Apollo musicke make; and Mars would be your man.
And, to be short, as much as Gods and men may doo,
So much your Highnesse here may finde, with faith and favour to.
But, if your noble mynde, resolved by decree,
Be not content by me *Desire* perswaded for to be,
Then, bends your willing eares unto my willing note,
And heare what song the Gods themselves have taught me now by
    rote.
Give eare, good gratious Queene, and so you shall perceive
That Gods in Heaven, and Men on Earth, are loath such Queenes to
    leave!

Herewith, the consort of musicke sounded, and *Deepedesire* sung this Song:—

> Come, Muses, come, and helpe me to lament;
> > Come woods, come waves, come hils, come doleful dales;
> Since life and death are both against me bent,
> > Come gods, come men, beare witnesse of my bales!
> O heavenly Nimphs, come helpe my heavy heart,
> With sighes to see Dame Pleasure thus depart!
>
> If death or dole could daunt a deepe desire,
> > If privie pangs could counterpeise my plaint,
> If tract of time a true intent could tire,
> > Or cramps of care a constant mind could taint,
> Oh, then might I at will here live and sterve,
> Although my deedes did more delight deserve.
>
> But out, alas! no gripes of greefe suffice
> > To break in twaine this harmlesse heart of mine;
> For, though delight be banisht from mine eies,
> > Yet lives *Desire*, whom paines can never pine.
> Oh, straunge affects! I live which seeme to die;
> Yet die to see my deere delight go by.
>
> Then, farewell sweet, for whom I taste such sower!
> > Farewell, delight, for whom I dwell in dole!
> Free will, farewell! farewell, my fancie's flower!
> > Farewell, content, whom cruell cares controle!
> Oh, farewell, life! delightfull death, farewell!
> I dye in heaven, yet live in darksome hell.

This Song being ended, the musicke ceased, and Silvanus concluded thus:

Most gratious Queene, as it should but evill have beseemed a God to be founde fraudulent or deceiptfull in his speech, so have I neither recompted nor foretolde anything unto your Majestie, but that which you have nowe founde true by experience; and, because the case is very lamentable in the conversion of *Deepedesire*, as also because they knowe that your Majestie is so highly favoured of the Gods, that they will not deny you any reasonable request; therfore, I do humbly crave in his behalfe, that you would either be a suter for him unto the heavenly powers, or else but onely to give your gracious consent that hee may be restored to his prystinate estate. Whereat, your Highnesse may be assured that heaven will smile, the earth will quake, men will clap their hands, and I will alwayes continue an humble beseecher for the flourishing estate of; your royall person; whom God, nowe and ever, preserve, to his good pleasure, and our great comfort.

AMEN!

TAM MARTI, QUAM MERCURIO.

Finis.

RALPH ROYSTER DOYSTER

A COMEDY,

ENTERED ON THE BOOKS OF THE STATIONERS' COMPANY,

1566.

NICHOLAS UDALL.

PROLEGOMENA.

In the year 1566, there was entered upon the Books of the Stationers' Company, a Notice of a Play about to be published, under the title of RAUF RUSTER DUSTER; but, no collector having ever been so fortunate as to procure a copy, it has always been supposed that the bookseller who made the entry, afterwards found reason to relinquish his intention of printing the piece in question. This conjecture, however, is now proved to have been unfounded, for, a copy was lately met with at a sale of old books, and is now deposited in the Library belonging to Eton College. Unfortunately, it wants the title-page, and the date of its publication cannot therefore be exactly ascertained; but there is little doubt that it was printed shortly after the above-mentioned Entry was made on the Stationers' Books; and, therefore, the justice of the claim of "Gammer Gurton's Needle" to be considered the first English. Comedy, is extremely questionable. No edition of the latter Play has been discovered of an earlier date than 1575; whilst the arguments adduced to prove that it was performed at Cambridge in 1566[89] are very inconclusive. Unless some more ancient copy of *Gammer Gurton* should hereafter be produced, the honour of priority must for the future be conceded to *Ralph Royster Doyster.*

The running-title of the original copy of this play is "Roisters Doister." *Roister,* or *Roisterer,* is a word frequently met with in the works of our early dramatists, where it signifies a riotous, dissipated brawler. The passage most in point which occurs to me, is in "The Returne from Pernassus," 1606, where *Judicio,* describing MARSTON, says of him—

> "He quaffs a cup of Frenchman's Helicon;
> "Then, royster doyster; in his oylie tearmes,
> "Cutts, thrusts, and foines at whomsoe'er he meets."

The word has not, even yet, fallen completely into disuse; and it will be acknowledged that *Ralph,* the hero of this play, does justice to his title, being as vain-glorious, swaggering a fool as heart could wish.

---

[89] Vide "Biog. Dram." Vol. I. Part ii. "Still."

That this play was written in the reign of Elizabeth, or in that of her predecessor, is shewn by passages in the first and last scenes, in which mention is made of the *Queen*. The scene of action, I imagine, is London, since *Truepenny*, in the 2nd Act, speaks of "the toppe of Paule's steeple." It must he confessed that the author, whoever he was, has introduced much sad trash, particularly in the 3rd Scene of Act 3; yet, it will I think be admitted that there is some humour displayed in several of the characters; and, without claiming for the composition all the comic merit which certain critics have affected to discover in "Gammer Gurton's Needle," it may at least be presumed that the thumps, kicks, and other practical jokes, which we now term buffoonery, highly amused the rude audiences for whose gratification they were intended. As a literary curiosity the play undoubtedly possesses great interest, and will form a valuable addition to the library of the dramatic amateur.

THE PROLOGUE.

WHAT creature is in health, either young or olde,
    But some mirth with modestie will be glad to use,
As we in this Enterlude shall now unfolde?
    Wherin all scurilitie we utterly refuse;
    Avoiding such mirth wherin is abuse
Knowing nothing more commendable for a man's recreation,
Than mirth which is used in an honest fashion.

For, mirth prolongeth lyfe, and causeth health;
    Mirth recreates our spirits, and voydeth pensivenesse;
Mirth increaseth amitie, (not hind'ring our wealth;)
    Mirth is to be used both of more and lesse,[90]
    Being mixed with virtue in decent comlynesse,
As we trust no good-nature can gainsaye the same:
Which mirth we intende to use, avoyding all blame.

The wyse poets, long time heretofore,
    Under merrie comedies, secretes did declare,
Wherein was contained very vertuous lore,
    With mysteries and forewarnings very rare.
    Such to write, neither Plautus nor Terence did spare,
Which among the learned at this day beares the bell:
These, with such other, therein dyd excell.

Our Comedie or Enterlude which we intende to play,
    Is named ROYSTER DOYSTER indeede,
Which against the vayne-glorious doth invey,
    Whose humour the roysting sort continually doth feede.
    Thus, by your patience, we intende to preceede
In this our Enterlude, by God's leave and grace:
And here I take my leave for a certain space.

---

[90] *of more and lesse.*] i.e. by rich and poor; or, by great and little.
"Both *more and less* have given him the revolt." *Macbeth*, Act V.

DRAMATIS PERSONÆ

RALPH ROYSTER DOYSTER ....*a Vain-glorious, Cowardly Blockhead.*
MATTHEW MERRYGREEK .... *a Needy Humorist.*
GAWYN GOODLUCK ....*a Merchant.*
TRISTRAM TRUSTY .... *Friend of Gawyn Goodluck.*
DOBINET DOUGHTY, ...*Servant of Ralph.*
HARPAX, ...*Servant of Ralph.*
TRUEPENNY .... *Servant of Dame Custance.*
SIM SURESBY ....*Servant of Gawyn Goodluck.*
A SCRIVENER.

DAME CHRISTIAN CUSTANCE, *a Widow, betrothed to Gawyn Goodluck.*
MADGE MUMBLECRUST, ...*Servant of Dame Custance.*
TIBET TALKAPACE, ...*Servant of Dame Custance.*
ANNOT ALYFACE, ...*Servant of Dame Custance.*

ACTUS j.   SCÆNA j.

MATHEWE MERYGREEKE. *(He entereth singing.)*

As long liveth the mery man (they say,)
As doth the sory man, and longer by a day;
Yet, the grassehopper, for all his sommer piping,
Sterveth in winter wyth hungrie gripyng:
Therefore, another sayd sawe doth men advise
That they be together both mery and wise.
This lesson must I practise, or else, ere long,
With me, Mathew Merygreeke, it will be wrong.
Indeede, men so call me, for, by him that us bought,
Whatever chaunce betide, I can take no thought.
Yet, wisedome woulde that I did myselfe bethinke
Where to be provided this day of meate and drinke;
For, know ye that, for all this merie note of mine,
He might appose me now, that should aske where I dine.
My lyving lyeth heere and there, of God's grace,
Sometime wyth this good man, sometyme in that place;
Sometime Lewis Loytrer biddeth me come neere;
Somewhyles Watkin Waster maketh me good cheere;
Sometime Davie Diceplayer (when he hath well cast)
Maketh revell route, as long as it will last;
Sometime Tom Titivile maketh us a feast;
Sometime with Sir Hugh Pie I am a bidden gueast;
Sometime at Nichol Neverthrive's I get a soppe;
Sometime I am feasted with Bryan Blinkinsoppe;
Sometime I hang on Hankyn Hoddidodie's sleeve;
But, this day on Ralff Royster Doystef's, by hys leeve:
For, truely, of all men he is my chiefe banker,
Both for meate and money, and my chiefe sheet-anker.
For, sooth, Royster Doyster in that he doth say,
And require what ye will, ye shall have no nay.
But now, of Royster Boyster somewhat to expresse,

That ye may esteeme him after his worthynesse,
In these twentie townes (and seeke them throughout)
Is not the like stocke whereon to grade a lout.
All the day long is be facing and craking[91]
Of his great actes in fighting and fray-making;
But, when Royster Doyster is put to his proofe,
To keep the Queene's peace is more for his behoofe.
If any woman smyle, or cast on hym an eye,
Up is he to the hard cares in love, by and bye;
And in alle the hotte haste must she be hys wyfe,
Else farewell hys good days, and farewell his lyfe:
Maister Raufe Royster Doyster is but dead and gon,
Except she on him take some compassion.
Then, chiefe of counsel must be Mathew Merygreeke,—
"What, if I for mariage to such an one seeke?"
Then must I sooth it, whatever it is;
For, what he sayth or doth cannot be amisse.
Holde by his yea and nay, be his nowne white sonne;[92]
Prayse and rouse him well, and ye have his heart wonne;
For, so well liketh he his owne fonde fashions,
That he taketh pride of false commendations.
But, such sporte have I with him, as I would not leese,
Though I should be bounde to lyve with bread and cheese.
For, exalt hym, and hav him as ye lust, indeede;
Yea, to hold his finger in a hole, for a neede.
I can with a worde make him fayne or loth;
I can with as much make him pleased or wroth;
I can, when I will, make him mery and glad;

---

[91] *Facing and craking*.] i. e. vaunting and boasting.

"You preserve
"A race of idle people here about you,
"*Facers* and talkers."
Maid's Tragedy, Act. 4.

[92] *White sonne*.] i.e his crony. *White-headed boy* is a common expression of fondness in Ireland, though the locks of the individual to whom it is applied may be "black as the raven's plume."

I can, when me lust, make him sory and sad;
I can set him in hope, and eke in dispaire;
I can make him speake rough, and make him speake fair.
But, I marvell I see him not all thys same day;
I will seeke him out. But, lo! he commeth thys way.
I have yond espied him sadly comming,
And in love, for twentie pounde, by his glommyng.

ACTUS j.   SCÆNA ij.

R. ROYSTER. — MATHEWE MERYGREEKE.

R. Royster. Come, death, when thou wilt, I am weary of my life.
M. Mery. *(Aside)* I told you I we should wowe another wife.
R. Royster. Why did God make me such a goodly person!
M. Mery. *(Aside.)* He is in, by the weke; we shall have sporte anon.
R. Royster. And where is my trustie friende, Mathew Merygreeke?
M. Mery. *(Aside.)* I wyll make as I sawe him not: he doth me seeke.
R. Royster. I have hym espied, me thinketh, yond is hee.—
Hough, Mathew Merygreeke, my friend, a word with thee.
M. Mery. I wyll not heare him, but make as I had haste. *(Aside.)*—
Farewell, all my good friendes, the tyme away doth waste;
And the tyde, they say, tarieth for no man.
R. Royster. Thou must, with thy good counsell, helpe me, if thou can.
M. Mery. God keepe thee, worshypfull Maister Royster Doyster,
And fare well the lustie Maister Royster Doyster.
R. Royster. I must needes speake with thee a worde or twaine.
M. Mery. Within a month or two I will be here againe.
Negligence in greate affaires, ye knowe, may marre all.
R. Royster. Attende upon me now, and well rewarde thee I shall.
M. Mery. I have taken my leave, and the tyde is well spent.
R. Royster. I die, except thou helpe; I pray thee be content.
Doe thy parte well now, and aske what thou wilt;
For, without thy aide, my matter is all spilt.
M. Mery. Then, to serve your turne, I will some paines take,

And let all myne owne affaires alone for your sake.

    R. Royster. My whole hope and trust resteth onely in thee.

    M. Mery. Then can ye not doe amise, whatever it be.

    R. Royster. Gramercies, Merygreeke, most bounde to thee I am.

    M. Mery. But, up with that heart, and speake out like a ramme;

Ye speake like a capon that had the cough now;

Bee of good cheere; anon ye shall doe well ynow.

    R. Royster. Upon thy comforte, I will all things well handle.

    M. Mery. So loe! that is a breath to blowe out a candle.[93]

But, what is this great matter? I woulde faine knowe;

We shall fynde remedie therefore, I trowe.

Doe ye lacke money? ye knowe myne olde offers:

Ye have always a key to my purse and coffers.

    R. Royster. I thanke thee; had ever man suche a frende!

    M. Mery. Ye gyve unto me: I must needes to you lende.

    R. Royster. Nay, I have money plentie, all things to discharge.

    M. Mery. (*Aside.*) That knewe I ryght well, when I made offer so large.

    R. Royster. But, it is no suche matter.

    M. Mery. What is it, than?

Are ye in daunger of debte to any man?

If ye be, take no thought, nor be not afraide;

Let them hardly take thought how they shall be paide.

    R. Royster. Tut, I owe nought.

    M. Mery. What then? feare ye imprisonment?

    R. Royster. No.

    M. Mery. No, I wist ye offende not so to be shent;

But, if ye had, the Toure coulde not you so holde,

But to break out at all times, ye woulde be bolde.

What is it? hath any man threatened you to beate?

    R. Royster. What is he that durst have put me in that heate?

He that beateth me, by his armes shall well finde

That I will not be farre from him, nor runne behinde.

    M. Mery. That thing knowe all men, ever since ye overthrewe

---

[93] The original reads—

        "So loe, that is a breast to blow out a candle."

The fellow of the lion which Hercules slewe.
But what is it than?

    R. Royster. Of love I make my mone.

    M. Mery. Ah, this foolishe love! wil't nea're let us alone?
But, bicause ye were refused the last day,
Ye sayd ye woulde ne're more be intangled that way.
I woulde medle no more, since I fynde all so unkinde.

    R. Royster. Yea, but I can not so put love but of my minde.

    M. Mery. But, is your love (tell me first, in any wise,)
In the way of mariage, or of merchandise?
If it may otherwise than lawfull be founde,
Ye get none of my helpe for an hundred pounde.

    R. Royster. No, by my trouthe, I woulde have hir to my wife.

    M. Mery. Then are ye a good man, and God save your life!
And what or who is she, with whom ye are in love?

    R. Royster. A woman, whome I knowe not by what meanes to move.

    M. Mery. Who is it?

    R. Royster. A woman yond.

    M. Mery. What is hir name?

    R. Royster. Hir yonder.

    M. Mery. Who?

    R. Royster. Mistresse, ah—

    M. Mery. Fy, fy for shame!
Love ye? and knowe not whome? but hir yonder,—a, woman?
We shall then get you a wyfe, I cannot tell whan.

    R. Royster. The faire woman that shipped with us yesternyght,
And I hearde hir name twice or thrice, and had it ryght.

    M. Mery. Yea, ye may see ye nere take me to good cheere with you,
If ye had, I coulde have tolde you hir name now.

    R. Royster. I was to blame indeede, but the nexte tyme perchaunce:
And she dwelleth in this house.

    M. Mery. What, Christian Custance?

    R. Royster. Except I have hir to my wife, I shall runne madde.

M. Mery. Nay, unwise perhaps; but, I warrant you for madde.[94]

R. Royster. I am utterly dead, unlesse I have my desire.

M. Mery. Where be the bellowes that blewe this sodeine fire?

R. Royster. I heare she is worthe a thousande pounde and more.

M. Mery. Yea, but learne this one lesson of me afore,

An hundred pounde of marriage money doubtlesse,

Is ever thirtie pounde sterlyng, or somewhat lesse,

So that hir thousande pounde, yf she be thriftie,

Is much neere aboute two hundred and fiftie,

Howbeit, wowers and widowes are never poore.

R. Royster. Is she a widowe? I love hir better therefore.

M. Mery. But I heare she hath made promise to another.

R. Royster. He shall goe without hir, and he were my brother.

M. Mery. I have hearde say, I am right well advised,

That she hath to Gawyn Goodlucke promised.

R. Royster. What is that Gawyn Goodlucke?

M. Mery. A merchant man.

R. Royster. Shall he speede afore me? Nay, Sir, by sweete Sainct Anne!

Ah Sir, Backare! quod Mortimer to his sowe,[95]

I will have hir myne owne selfe, I make God a vow.

For, I tell thee, she is worthe a thousande pounde.

M. Mery. Yet, a fitter wife for your maship[96] might be founde;

Suche a goodly man as you might get one wyth lande,

Besides poundes of golde a thousande and a thousande,

And a thousande, and a thousande, and a thousande,

And so to the summe of twentie hundred thousand:—

Your most goodly personage is worthie of no lesse.

R. Royster. I am sorie God made me so comely, doubtlesse;

For, that maketh me eche were so highly favoured,

---

[94] *For madde.*] It is scarcely necessary to remark, that *for* is, constantly used in the sense of *from* by our early writers.

[95] This was a proverbial expression. See several instances of its use cited in a Note on the "Taming of the Shrew," Act. ii. Sc. 1. in Reed's Shakspeare. *Backare* means *Give place!* or *Go back!*

[96] *Your maship.*] i. e. your mastership.

And all women on me so enamoured.
    M. Mery. Enamoured quod you? have ye spied out that?
Ah, Sir, mary nowe I see you know what is what.
Enamoured ka? mary, Sir, say that againe,
But I thought not I ye had marked it so plaine.
    R. Royster. Yes, eche where they gaze all upon me, and stare.
    M. Mery. Yea, Malkyn, I warrant you, as muche as they dare.
And ye will not beleve what they say in the streete,
When your mashyp passeth by, all suche as I meete,
That sometimes I can scarce finde what answere to make.
"Who is this (sayth one) Sir Launcelot da Lake?"
"Who is this, greate Guy of Warwicke," sayth another?
"No, (say I) it is the thirteenth Hercules' brother."
"Who is this? noble Hector of Troy?" sayth the thirde:
"No, but of the same nest (say I) it is a birde."
"Who is this? greate Goliah, Sampson, or Colbrande?"
"No, (say I) but it is a brute of the Alie lande."
"Who is this? greate Alexander? or Charle le Maigne?
"No, it is the tenth Worthie," say I to them agayne:
I knowe not if I sayd well—
    R. Royster. Yes, for so I am.
    M. Mery. Yea, for there were but nine Worthies before ye came.
To some others, the thirde Cato I doe you call;
And so, as well as I can, I answere them all.
"Sir, I pray you what lorde or great gentleman is this?"
"Maister Ralph Royster Doyster, dame, (say I) y'wis."
"O Lorde, (sayth she than) what a goodly man it is,
Woulde Christ I had such a husbande as he is."
"O Lorde, (say some) that the sight of his face we lacke:'
"It is inough for you (say I) to see his backe.
His face is for ladies of high and noble parages,
With whome he hardly scapeth great mariages."
With muche more than this, and much otherwise.

R. Royster. I con thee thanke,[97] that thou canst suche answeres devise:
But, I perceyve thou doste me throughly knowe.

    M. Mery. I marke your maners for myne owne learnyng, I trowe.
But suche is your beautie, and suche are your actes,
Suche is your personage, and suche are your factes,[98]
That all women, faire and fowle, more or lesse,
They eye you, they lubbe you, they talke of you doubtlesse.
Your pleasant looke maketh them all merie,
Ye passe not by, but they laugh till they be werie;
Yea, and money coulde I have, the truthe to tell,
Of many, to bring you that way where they dwell.

    R. Royster. Merygreeke, for this thy reporting well of me—

    M. Mery. What shoulde I else, sir? it is my duetie, pardee.

    R. Royster. I promise thou shalt not lacke, while I have a grote.

    M. Mery. Faith sir, and I ne're had more neede of a newe cote.

    R. Royster. Thou shalt have one tomorrowe, and golde for to spende.

    M. Mery. Then, I trust to bring the day to a goode ende.
For, as for myne owne parte, having money inowe,
I coulde lyve onely with the remembrance of you.
But nowe to your widowe, whome you love so hotte.

    R. Royster. By cocke, thou sayest truthe, I had almost forgotte.

    M. Mery. What, if Christian Custance will not have you, what?

    R. Royster. Have me? yes I warrant you, never doubt of that.
I knowe she loveth me, but she dare not speake.

    M. Mery. Indeede, meete it were somebody should it breake.

    R. Royster. She looked on me twenty tymes yesternight,
And laughed so.

    M. Mery. That she coulde not sitte upright.

---

[97] *I con thee thanke.*] The original has—"I *can*," &c. but, the expression to *con*, i. e. to *give* thanks, is so common in the works of the old dramatists, that I have no doubt the true reading is restored. So in "Wily Beguiled," 1606—

    "I *con* Master Churms *thanks* for it."

[98] *Factes.*] i. e. feats or deeds, from the Latin factum—

    "And rattle forth his *facts* of war and blood."

            Tamburlaine the Great, Part i. 1590.

R. Royster. No, faith, coulde she not.

M. Mery. No, even such a thing I cast.

R. Royster. But, for wowyng, thou knowest, women are shamefast.
But, and she knewe my minde, I knowe she would be glad,
And thinke it the best chaunce that ever she had.

M. Mery. To hir, then, like a man, and be bolde forthe to starte,
Wowers never speede well that have a false harte.

R. Royster. What may I best doe?

M. Mery. Sir, remaine ye a while [here.]⁹⁹
Ere long one or other of hir house will appere.
Ye knowe my minde.

R. Royster. Yea, now hardly lette me alone.

M. Mery. In the mean time, Sir, if you please, I wyll home,
And call your musitians; for, in this your case,
It woulde sette you forth, and all your wowyng grace.
Ye may not lacke your instrumentes to play and sing.

R. Royster. Thou knowest I can doe that.

M. Mery. As well as any thing.
Shall I go call your folkes, that we may shewe a cast?

R. Royster. Yea, runne, I beseeche thee, in all possible haste.

M. Mery. I goe.   [*Exeat.*

R. Royster. Yea, for I love singyng, out of measure,
It comforteth my spirites, and doth me great pleasure.
But who commeth forth yond, from my swete-hearte Custance?
My matter frameth well, thys is a luckie chaunce.

ACTUS j.   SCÆNA iij.

MAGE MUMBLECRUST *spinning on the distaffe* — TIBET TALKAPACE
   sowyng — ANNOT ALYFACE *knittyng.* — R. ROYSTER.

M. Mumbl. If thys distaffe were spoone, Margerie Mumblecrust—
Tib. Talk. Where good stale ale is, will drinke no water I trust.

---

⁹⁹ The word in brackets is not in the original.

M. Mumbl. Dame Custance hath promised us good ale and white bread.

Tib. Talk. If she keep not promise, I will beshrewe hir head.
But it will be starke night before I shall have done.

R. Royster. I will stande here awhile, and talke with them anon.
I heare them speake of Custance, which doth my heart good;
To hear hir name spoken, doth even comfort my blood.

M. Mumbl. Sit down to your worke, Tibet, like a good girle.

Tib. Talk. Nourse, medle you with your spyndle and your whirle.
No haste but good, Madge Mumblecrust; for, whip and whurre,[100]
The old proverb doth say, never made good furre.

M. Mumbl. Well, ye wyll sitte downe to your worke, anon, I trust.

Tib. Talk. Soft fire maketh sweete malte, good Madge Mumblecrust.

M. Mumbl. And sweete malte maketh joly good ale for the nones.

Tib. Talk. Which will slide downe the lane without any bones.

[Cantet.[101]

Old browne-bread crustes must have much good mumbling;
But, good ale downe your throte hath good easie tumblyng.

R. Royster. The jolyest wenche that ere I hearde, little mouse;
May I not rejoice that she shall dwell in my house?

Tib. Talk. So, Sirrha,[102] nowe this geare beginneth for to frame.

M. Mumbl. Thanks to God, though your work stand stil, your tong is not
    lame.

Tib. Talk. And though your teeth be gone, both so sharpe and so fine,
Yet your tongue can renne on patins as well as mine.

M. Mumbl. Ye were not for nought named Tyb Talke apace.

Tib. Talk. Doth my talke grieve you? Alack, God save our grace!

M. Mumbl. I holde a grote, ye will drinke anon for this geare.

Tib. Talk. And I wyll not, pray you the stripes for me to beare.

---

[100] *Whurre.*] i. e. scolding.—"*Whur*, to snarl like a dog."—*Bailey.*

[101] The Songs introduced in our old plays are seldom found in the printed copies. Some of those sung in this piece are, however, given at the end. In the above instance, the choice of a song was probably left to the discretion of the performer.

[102] *Sirrha.*] The terms *Sirrah* and *Sir* appear to have been formerly applied indifferently both to male and female. In "Promos and Cassandra," 1578, *Grymball* says to his mistress—
    "Ah, *syr*, you woulde, belike, let my cocke-sparrowes go."

M. Mumbl. I holde a penny, ye will drinke without a cup.

Tib. Talk. Wherein so ere ye drinke, I wote ye drinke all up.

An. Alyface. By Cock,[103] and well sowed, my good Tibet Talkeapace.

Tib. Talk. And e'en as well knitte, my nowne Annot Alyface.

R. Royster. See what a sort she kepeth that must be my wife.
Shall not I, when I have hir, leede a merrie life?

Tib. Talk. Welcome, my good wenche, and sitte here by me just.

An. Alyface. And howe doth our olde beldame here, Mage Mumblecrust?

Tib. Talk. Chydes, and findes fault, and threatens to complaine.

An. Alyface. To make us poore girles shent; to hir is small gaine.

M. Mumbl. I did neither chyde, nor complaine, nor threaten.

R. Royster. It woulde grieve my heart to see one of them beaten.

M Mumbl. I dyd nothyng but byd hir work and holde hir peace.

Tib. Talk. So woulde I, if you coulde your clattering cease:
But the devill cannot make old trotte holde hir tong.

An Alyface. Let all these matters passe, and we three sing a song;
So shall we pleasantly both the tyme beguile now,
And eke dispatche all our workes, ere we can tell how.

Tib. Talk. I 'shrew them that say nay, and that shall not be I.

M. Mumbl. And I am well content.

Tib. Talk. Sing on then by and by.

R. Royster. And I will not away, but listen to their song;
Yet, Merygreeke and my folkes tary very long.

Tib. An. and Margerie doe singe here.
Pipe, mery Annot; &c.
Trilla, Trilla, Trillarie.
Worke, Tibet; worke, Annot; worke, Margerie;
Sewe, Tibet; knitte, Annot; spinne, Margerie;
Let us see who will winne the victorie.

Tib. Talk. This sleeve is not willing to be sewed, I trowe,
A small thing might make me all in the grounde to throwe.

---

[103] *By Cock.*] A corruption of the sacred name.

151

Then they sing agayne.
Pipe, merrie Annot; &c.
Trilla, Trilla, Trillarie.
What, Tibet! what, Annot! what, Margerie!
Ye sleepe, but we doe not, that shall we trie;
Your fingers be nombde, our worke will not lie.

Tib. Talk. If ye do so againe, well; I would advise you nay.
In good sooth, one stoppe more, and I make holy day.
They sing the thirde tyme.
Pipe, merry Annot; &c.
Trilla, Trilla, Trillarie.
Nowe Tibbet, now Annot, now Margerie;
Nowe whippet apace for the maystrie;
But it will not be, our mouth is so drie.

Tib. Talk. Ah, eche finger is a thombe to day me thinke,
I care not to let all alone, choose it swimme or sinke.

They syng the fourth tyme.
Pipe, mery Annot; &c.
Trilla, Trilla, Trillarie.
When, Tibet? when, Annot? when, Margerie?
I will not,—I can not,—no more can I.
Then, give we all over, and there let it lye!
Lette hir cast downe hir worke.

Tib. Talk. There it lieth, the worste is but a curried cote,
But I am used thereto, I care not a grote.
An. Alyface. Have we done syngyng since? then will I in againe,
Here I founde you, and here I leave both twaine.
Exeat.

M. Mumbl. And I will not be long after: Tib. Talkapace.
Tib. Talk. What is the matter?
M. Mumbl. Yond stode a man al this space,

And hath hearde al that ever we spake together.

   Tib. Talk. Mary, the more loute he for his comming hither.

And the lesse good he can to listen to maidens' talke.

I care not, and I goe byd him hence for to walke:

It were well done to knowe what he maketh here away.

   R. Royster. Now myght I speake to them, if I wist what to say.

   M. Mumbl. Nay, we will go bath of's, and see what he is.

   R. Royster. One that hearde all your talke and synging y'wis.

   Tib. Talk. The more to blame you; a good thriftie husbande

Woulde elsewhere have had some better matters in hande.

   R. Royster. I did it for no harme; but for good love I beare

To your dame Mistresse Custance, I did your talke heare.

And, mistresse Nourse, I will kisse you for acquaintance.

   M. Mumbl. I come anon, sir.

   Tib. Talk. Faith, I woulde our dame Custance

Sawe this geare.

   M. Mumbl. I must first wipe al cleane, yea I must.

   Tib. Talk. Ill chieve it dotyng foole, but it must be cust.

   M. Mumbl. God yelde you, sir; chad not so much, I chotte not whan;

Nere since chwas born, chwine,[104] of such gay gentleman.

   R. Royster. I will kisse you too, mayden, for the good will I beare ye.

   Tib. Talk. No, forsooth, by your leave, ye shall not kisse me.

   R. Royster. Yes, he not afearde, I doe not disdayne you a whit;

   Tib. Talk. Why should I feare you? I have not so little wit;

Ye are but a man, I know very well.

   R. Royster. Why, then?

   Tib. Talk. Forsooth, for I wyll not, I use not to kisse men.

   R. Royster. I would faine kisse you too, good maiden, if I myght.

   Tib. Talk. What shold that neede?

   R. Royster. But to honor you, by this light.

I use to kisse all them that I love, to God I vowe.

   Tib. Talk. Yea sir? I pray you, when dyd ye last kisse your cowe?

   R. Royster. Ye might be proude to kisse me, if ye were wise.

---

[104] *i.e.* I had not so much, I wot not when: never since I was born, I ween.

Tib. Talk. What promotion were therein?

R. Royster. Nourse is not so nice.

Tib. Talk. Well, I have not been taught to kissing and licking.

R. Royster. Yet, I thanke you, mistresse Nourse, ye made no sticking.

M. Mumbl. I will not sticke for a kisse, with such a man as you.

Tib. Talk. They that lust: I will againe to my sewyng now.

Re-enter ANOT ALYFACE.

An. Alyface. Tidings hough, tidings! dame Custance greeteth you well.

R. Royster. Whome me?

An. Alyface. You Sir? No, Sir. I do no suche tale tell.

R. Royster. But, and she knewe me here.

An. Algface. Tibet Talkapace,
Your Mistresse Custance, and mine, must speake with your grace.

Tib. Talk. With me?

An. Alyface. You must come in to hir, out of all doutes.

Tib. Talk. And my work not half done! a mischief on all loutes!

Ex. am.

R. Royster. Ah good sweet Nourse.

M. Mumbl. A good sweete gentleman.

R. Royster. Who?[105]

M. Mumbl. Nay, I can not tel Sir, but what thing would you?

R. Royster Howe dothe sweete Custance, my heart of gold, tell me how?

M. Mumbl. She dothe very well Sir, and commaundes me to you.

R. Royster. To me?

M. Mumbl. Yea, to you Sir.

R. Royster. To me? Nurse, tell me plain,
To me?

M. Mumbl. Yea.

R. Royster. That word maketh me alive again.

M. Mumbl. She commanded me to one, last day, who ere it was.

R. Royster. That was e'en to me, and none other, by the Masse.

---

[105] The original has "*What?*"—The alteration is made both *rhythmi gratia,* and to amend the sense.

154

M. Mumbl. I can not tell you surely, but one it was.

R. Royster. It was I, and none other:—this commeth to good passe.
I promise thee, Nourse, I favour hir.

M. Mumbl. E'en so, Sir.

R. Royster. Bid hir sue to me for mariage.

M. Mumbl. E'en so, Sir.

R. Royster. And surely for thy sake she shall speeds.

M. Mumbl. E'en so, Sir.

R. Royster. I shall be contented to take hir.

M. Mumbl. E'en so, Sir.

R. Royster. But at thy request, and for thy sake.

M. Mumbl. E'en so, Sir.

R. Royster. And, come, harke in thine eare what to say

M. Mumbl. E'en so, Sir.

Here lette him tell hir a great long tale in hir eare.

ACTUS j.   SCÆNA iiij.

MATHEW MERYGREEKE — DOBINET DOUGHTIE — HARPAX
— RALPH ROYSTER — MARGERIE MUMBLECRUST.

M. Mery. Come on, Sirs, apace, and quite yourselves like men.
Your pains shall be rewarded.

D. Dough. But, I wot not when.

M. Mery. Do your Maister worship, as ye have done in time past.

D. Dough. Speake to them: of mine office he shall have a cast.

M. Mery. Harpax, looke that thou doe well too, and thy fellow.

Harpaix. I warrant, if he will myne example followe.

M. Mery. Curtsie, whoresons! douke you and crouche at every worde.

D. Dough. Yes, whether our Maister speake earnest or borde.[106]

---

[106] *Borde.*] *i. e.* jokingly.—*Borde, bourd,* or *boord,* as the word is spelled by Spenser, means
to jest or sport; from the French *Bourder.*—"*Bourd* neither with me nor my honour," is a
common North-Country saying.

M. Mery. For, upon this lieth[107] his preferment in deede.

D. Dough. Oft is he a wower, but never doth he speede.

M. Mery. But, with whome is he now so sadly roundyng[108] yond?

D. Dough. With *Nobs Nicebecetur Miserere* fonde.

M. Mery. God be at your wedding, be ye spedde alreadie?
I did not suppose that your love was so greedie.
I perceive nowe ye have chose of devotion,
And joy have ye, ladie, of your promotion.

R. Royster. Tushe, foole, thou art deceived, this is not she.

M. Mery. Well, make muche of hir, and keepe hir well, I 'vise ye.
I will take no charge of such a faire piece keeping.

M. Mumbl. What ayleth this fellow? he driveth me to weeping.

M. Mery. What, weepe on the wedding day? be merrie woman,
Though I say it, ye have chose a good gentleman.

R. Royster. Kock's nownes,[109] what meanest thou man? tut, a whistle.

M. Mery. Ah Sir, be good to hir, she is but a gristle!
Ah sweete lambe and coney.

R. Rogster. Tut, thou art deceived.

M. Mery. Weepe no more, lady, ye shall be well received.
Up with some mery noyse, Sirs,[110] to bring home the bride!

R. Royster. Gog's armes,[111] knave, art thou madde? I tell thee thou art wide.

M. Ellery. Then, ye entende by nyght to have hir home brought.

R. Royster. I tell thee, no.

M. Mery. How then?

R. Royster. 'Tis neither meant ne thought.

M. Mery. What shall we then doe with hir?

R. Royster. Ah foolish harebraine,
This is not she.

---

[107] The original reads—"For this lieth upon."

[108] *Roundying.*] i.e. whispering.

   "And in his ear him *rounded* close behind."

       Faerie Queene, Book 3, Canto 1o.

[109] *Koch's nownes.*] i. e. God's bones. Vide Note 103.

[110] *Noise.*] This word was anciently put for *music.*

[111] *Gog's armes.*] i. e. God's arms. Vide Notes 103 and 109.

M. Mery. No, is [it not?][112] Why then unsayde again:
And what yong girle is this with your mashyp so bolde?

R. Royster. A girle?

M. Mery. Yea, I dare say, scarse yet three score yere olde.

R. Royster. This same is the faire widowe's Nourse, of whome ye wotte.

M. Mery. Is she but a Nourse of a house? hence home, olde trotte!
Hence, at once.

R. Royster. No, No.

M. Mery. What, an please your maship,
A nourse talke so homely with one of your worship?

R. Royster. I will have it so: it is my pleasure and will.

M. Mery. Then I am content. Nourse, come againe, tarry still.

R. Royster. What, she will helpe forward this my sute, for hir part.

M. Mery. Then is't mine own pygsnie, and blessing on hir hart.

R. Royster. This is our best frend, man.

M. Mery. Then teach hir what to say.

M. Mumbl. I am taught alreadie.

M. Mery. Then go, make no delay.

R. Royster. Yet hark, one worde in thine eare.

M. Mery. Back, Sirs, from his taile!

R. Royster. Back, vilaynes; will ye be privie of my counsaile?

M. Mery. Backe, Sirs, so: I tolde you afore, ye woulde be shent.[113]

R. Royster. She shall have the first day a whole pecke of argent.

M. Mumbl. A pecke! *Namine Patris*, have ye so much [to][114] spare?

R. Royster. Yea, and a cart lode thereto, or else were it bare;
Besides other movables, housholde-stuffe and lande.

M. Mumbl. Have ye lands too?

R. Royster. An hundred marks.

M. Mery. Yea, a thousand.

M. Mumbl. And have ye cattel too, and sheepe too?

R. Royster. Yea, a fewe.

M. Mery. He is ashamed the numbre of them to shewa.

---

[112] The words within brackets are added.

[113] *Shent.*] i.e. scolded.

[114] The word within brackets is added.

E'en rounde about him, as many thousande sheepe goes,
As he and thou and I too have fingers and toes.

    M. Mumbl. And how many yeares olde be you?

    R. Royster. Fortie at lest.

    M. Mery. Yea, and thrice fortie to them.

    R. Royster. Nay, now thou dost jest.

I am not so olde, thou misreckonest my yeares.

    M. Mery. I know that: but my minde was on bullockes and steeres.

    M. Mumbl. And what shall I shewe hir your mastership's name is?

    R. Royster. Nay, she shall make sute, ere she shall know that y'wis.

    M. Mumbl. Yet, let me somewhat knowe.

    M. Mery. This is hee, understand

That killed the blue spider in Blanchepouder lande.

    M. Mumbl. Yea, Jesus William, zee law! dyd he zo, law?

    M. Mery. Yea, and the last elephant that ever he sawe,

As the beast passed by, he start out of a buske,[115]

And e'en with pure strength of armes pluckt out his great tuske.

    M. Mumbl. Jesus, *Nomine Patris*, what a thing was that!

    R. Royster. Yea, but Merygreeke, one thing thou hast forgot.

    M. Mery. What?

    R. Royster. Of another elephant.

    M. Mery. Oh, hym that fledde away?

    Royster. Yea.

    M. Mery. Yea, he knewe that his match was in place that day.

Tut, he bet the king of crickets on Christmasse day,

That he crept in a hole, and not a worde to say.

    M. Mumbl. A sore man, by Zembletee.

    M. Mery. Why, he wrong a club,

Once in a fray, out of the handes of Belzebub.

    R. Royster. And how when Mumfision—

    M. Mery. Oh your Cousterlyng,

Bore the lanterne a-fielde so before the gozelyng ——

Nay, that is too long a matter now to be tolde.

---

[115] *Buske*] i. e. a copse or bush; from *Boscus*.
"And every *bosky* bourn from side to side."—*Milton*.

Never aske his name, Nourse, I warrant thee, be bolde;
He conquered in one day from Rome to Naples,
And wonne townes, Nourse, as fast as thou canst make apples.
 M. Mumbl. Oh Lorde, my heart quaketh for fear, he is so sore.
 R. Royster. Thou makest hir too much afearde, Merygreeke; no more.
This tale woulde feare my sweete heart Custance right evill.
 M. Mery. Nay, let hir take him, Nurse, and feare not the devil.
But, thus is our song dasht. Sirs, ye may home againe.
 R. Royster. No, shall they not. I charge you all, here remaine!
The villaine slaves, a whole day, are they can be founde.
 M. Mery. Couche on your marybones, whoresons, down to the ground.
Was it meete he should tarie so long in one place,
Without harmonie of musike, or some solace?
Whoso hath suche bees as your maister in hys head,
Had neede to have his spirites with musike be fed.—
By your maistership's licence.
 R. Royster. What is that? a moate?
 M. Mery. No, it was a foole's feather had light on your coate.
 R. Royster. I was nigh no feathers, since I came from my bed.
 M. Mery. No sir, it was a haire that was fall from your hed.
 R. Royster. My men com when it plese them.
 M. Mery. By your leve.
 R. Royster. What is that?
 M. Mery. Your gowne was foule spotted with the foot of a gnat.
 R. Royster. Their maister to offend they are nothing afearde.
What now?
 M. Mery. A lousy haire from your maistership's beard.
 Omnes Famuli. And sir, for Nurse's sake, pardon this one offence.
We shall not after this shew the like negligence.
 R. Royster. I pardon you this once; and come, sing ne're the wurse.
 M. Mery. How like you the goodnesse of this gentleman, Nurse?
M. Mumbl. God save his maistership, that can so his men forgeve;
And I wyll heare them sing ere I go, by his leave.
 R. Royster. Mary, and thou shalt, wenche; come, we two will daunce.
 M. Mumbl. Nay, I will by mine owne selfe foote the song, perchaunce.

R. Royster. Go it, Sirs, lustily.

M. Mumbl. Pipe up a mery note,
Let me heare it playde, I will foote it for a grote.   [*Cantent.*[116]

R. Royster. Now, Nurse, take thys same letter here to thy mistresse;
And as my trust is in thee, plie my businesse.

M. Mumbl. It shal be done.

M. Mery. Who made it?

R. Royster. I wrote it ech whit.

M. Mery. Then nedes it no mending.

M. Mery. No, I know your wit.

R. Royster. I warrant it wel.

M. Mumbl. It shall be delivered;
But, if ye speede, shall I be considered?

M. Mery. Whough, dost thou doubt of that?

M. Mumbl. What shall I have?

M. Mery. An hundred times more than thou canst devise to crave.

M. Mumbl. Shall I have some newe geare? for my olde is all spent.

M. Mery. The worst kitchen wench shall goe in ladies' rayment.

M. Mumbl. Yea?

M. Mery. And the worst drudge in the house shal go better
Than your mistresse doth now.

M. Mumbl. Then I trudge with your letter.

R. Royster. Now may I repose me: Custance is mine owne.
Let us sing and play homeward, that it may be knowne.

M. Mery. But, are you sure that your letter is well enough?

R. Royster. I wrote it myselfe.

M. Mery. Then sing we to dinner.

[*Here they sing, and go out singing.*

---

[116] The Song will be found at the end of the Play.

<h1 style="text-align:center">ACTUS j.   SCÆNA v.</h1>

CHRISTIAN CUSTANCE — MARGERIE MUMBLECRUST.

C. Custance. Who tooke thee thys letter, Margerie Mumblecrust?

M. Mumbl. A lustie gay bachelor tooke it me of trust,
And if ye seeke to him, he will love your doing.

C. Custance. Yea, but where learned he that manner of wowing?

M. Mumbl. If to sue to him, you will any paines take,
He will have you to hys wife (he sayth) for my sake.

C. Custance. Some wise gentleman belike: I am bespoken:
And I thought verily thys had bene some token
From my dere spouse,[117] Gawin Goodlucke, whom, when him please,
God luckily send home, to both our heartes' ease!

M. Mumbl. A joyly man it is, I wote well by report,
And would have you to him for marriage resort:
Best open the writing, and see what it doth speake.

C. Custance. At thys time, Nourse, I will neither reade ne breake.

M. Mumbl. He promised to give you a whole peeke of golde.

C. Custance. Perchaunce, lacke of a pynte, when it shal be all tolde.

M. Mumbl. I would take a gay riche husbande, and I were you.

C. Custance. In good sooth, Madge, e'en so would I, if I were thou.[118]
But, no more of this fonde talke now, let us go in;
And see thou no more move me folly to begin;
Nor bring me no mo letters, for no man's pleasure,
But thou know from whom.

M. Mumbl. I warrant ye shall be sure.

---

[117] *From my dear spouse.*] The word *spouse* is here used for *lover*, since it appears from other passages that she was only affianced to Goodluck.

[118] The idea is borrowed from Alexander's celebrated reply to Parmenio.

ACTUS ij.   SCENA i.

DOBINET DOUGHTIE.

Where is the house I goe to, before or behinde?
I know not where, nor when, nor how I shall it find.
If I had ten mens' bodies, and legs, and strength,
This trotting that I have, must needes lame me at length.
And now that my maister is new set on wowing
I trust[119] there shall none of us finde lacke of doing:"
Two paire of shoes a day will nowe be too little
To serve me, I must trotte to and fro so mickle.
"Go beare me thys token; carrie me this letter;"
Nowe this is the best way; nowe that way is better.
"Up before day, sirs, I charge you, an houre or twaine;
"Trudge, do me thys message, and bring worde quicke againe."
If one misse but a minute, then, his armes and woundes,
"I woulde not have slacked for ten thousand poundes.
"Nay see, I beseeche yon, if my most trustie page
"Goe not now about to hinder my marriage."
So fervent hotte wowyng, and so farre from wiving,
I trowe never was any creature livyng;
With every woman is he in some love's pang;
Then up to our lute at midnight, twangledome twang.
Then twang with our sonets, and twang with our dumps,[120]
And heyhough from our heart, as heavy as lead lumpes.
Then to our recorder,[121] with toodleoodle poope,
As the howlet out of an yvie bushe should hoope.
Anon to our gitterne,[122] thrumpledum thrumpledum thrum,
Thrumpledum, thrumpledum, thrumpledum, thrumpledum, thrum.

---

[119] *I trust.*] i. e. I trow.

[120] *Our dumps.*] A dump is a tune: generally a mournful one.

[121] *Our recorder.*] i. e. a flageolet.

[122] *Our gitterne.*] A gitterne, citterne, or cithern, as the word is variously spelled, is a lute or guitar. It is derived from *cithara*.

Of songs and balades also he is a maker,
And that can he as finely doe as Jacke Raker;
Yea, and extempore will he ditties compose;
Foolishe Marsias nere made the like I suppose;
Yet must we sing them, as good stuffe I undertake,
As for such a penman is well fittyng to make.
"Ah, for these long nights; hey how, when will it be day?
"I feare ere I come, she will be wowed away."
Then, when aunswere is made, that it may not bee,
"O death, why commest thou not?" by and by, sayth he.
But then, from his heart to put away sorowe,
He is as farre in with some news love next morowe.
But, in the meane season, we trudge and we trot,
From dayspring to midnight, I sit not, nor rest not.
And now am I sent to dame Christian Custance;
But I feare it will ende with a mock for pastance.[123]
I bring hir a ring, with a token in a cloute,
And by all gesse, this same is hir house out of doute.
I knowe it now perfect, I am in my right way.
And loe, yond the olde Nourse, that was wyth us last day.

ACTUS ij.   SCENA ij.

MAGE MUMBLECRUST — DOBINET DOUGHTIE.

M. Mumbl. I was nere so shoke up afore, since I was borne.
That our mistresse coulde not have chid, I wold have sworne;
And I pray God I die, if I ment any harme;
But, for my life time this shall be to me a charme.
D. Dough. God you save and see, Nurse; and howe is it with you?

---

[123] *For pastance.*] i. e. for sport. So in Act 4, Scene 6.
"Do ye think, Dame Custance,
"That in this wowing I have ment ought but *pastance*?"
Again, Act 5, Scene 2.
"Truly, most dear spouse, nought was done but for *pastance.*"

M. Mumbl. Mary, a great deale the worse it is, for suche as thou.

D. Dough. For me? Why so?

M. Mumbl. Why, wer not thou one of them, say,

That song and playde here with the gentleman last day?

D. Dough. Yes, and he would know if you have for him spoken.

And prayes you to deliver this ring and token.

M. Mumbl. Nowe, by the token that God tokened, brother,

I will deliver no token [for]¹²⁴ one nor other.

I have once ben so shent for your maister's pleasure,

As I will not be agayne for all hys treasure.

D. Dough. He will thanke you woman.

M. Mumbl. I will none of his thanke.   [*Ex.*

D. Dough. I weene I am a prophete; this geare will prove blanke.

But what, should I home againe without answere go?

It were better go to Rome on my head, than so.

I will tary here this moneth, but some of the house

Shall take it of me, and then I care not a louse.

But yonder commeth forth a wenche or a ladde,

If he have not one Lumbarde's touche, my lucke is bad.

ACTUS ij.   SCENA iij.

TRUEPENIE — D. DOUGH.

Trupenie. I am cleane lost for lacke of mery companie;

We 'gree not halfe so well within, our wenches and I;

They will commaunde like mistresses, they will forbyd;

If they be not served, Truepenie must be chyd.

Let them be as mery nowe, as you can desire,

With turnyng of a hande, our mirth lieth in the mire.

I can not skill of such chaungeable mettle,

---

¹²⁴ The word within brackets is added.

There is nothing with them but "In dock, out nettle."[125]

    D. Dough. Whether is it better that I speake to him furst,
Or he first to me? It is good to cast the wurst.
If I beginne first, he will smell all my purpose,
Otherwise I shall not neede any thyng to disclose.

    Truepanie. What boy have we yonder? I will see what he is.

    D. Dough. He commeth to me. It is hereabout, y'wis.

    Trupenie. Wouldest thou ought, friende, that thou lookest so about?

    D. Dough. Yea; but whether ye can helpe me or no, I dout.
I seeke to one Mistresse Custance' house, here dwellyng.

    Trupenie. It is my mistresse ye seeke to, by your telling.

    D. Dough. Is there any of that name heere but shee?

    Trupenie. Not one in all the whole towne that I knowe, pardee.

    D. Dough. A widowe she is, I trow.

    Trupenie. And what and she be?

    D. Dough. But ensured to an husbande.

    Trupenie. Yea, so thinke we.

    D. Dough. And I dwell with hir husbande that trusteth to be.

    Trupenie. In faith then must thou needes be welcome to me.
Let us, for acquaintance, shake hands togither,
And, what ere thou be, heartily welcome hither.

Enter TIB. TALKAPACE *and* ANOT ALYFACE.

    Tib. Talk. Well, Trupenie, never but flinging.

    An Alyface. And frisking?

    Trupenie, Well, Tibet and Annot, still swingyng and whiskyng?

    Tib. Talk. But, ye roile abroade.

    An. Alyface. In the streete everie where.

    Trupenie. Where are ye twaine? in chamhers, when ye mete me there?
But, come hither, fooles; I have one nowe by the hande,
Servant to hym that must be our mistresse' husbande;

---

[125] A proverbial expression. It is still a common practice for superstitious country-folks, when stung by a nettle, to rub with a dock-leaf the part affected, at the same time repeating the words in a text.

165

Byd him welcome.

 An. Alyface. To me truly is he welcome.

 Tib. Talk. Forsooth! and, as I may say, heartily welcome.

 D. Dough. I thank you, mistresse maides.

 An. Alyface. I hope we shall better know.

 Tib. Talk. And, when will our new master come?

 D. Dough. Shortly, I trow.

 Tib. Talk. I woulde it were to-morrowe; for, till he resorte,

Our mistresse, being a widowe, hath small comforte;

And, I hearde our Nourse speake of an husbande to-day,

Ready for our mistresse; a rich man and a gay.

And we shall go in our Frenche hoodes every day;

In our silke cassocks (I warrant you) freshe and gay;

In our tricke ferdegews, and billiments of golde;

Brave in our sutes of chaunge, seven double folde.

Then shall ye see Tibet, sirs, treade the mosse so trimme;

Nay, why sayd I treade? ye shall see hir glide and swimme;

Not lumperdee, clumperdee, like our spaniell Rig.

 Trupenie. Mary, then, prickmedaintie; come, toste me a fig.

Who shall then know our Tib Talkeapace, trow ye?

 An. Alyface. And why not Annot Alyface as fyne as she?

 Trupenie. And what had Tom Truepenie, a father or none?

 An. Alyface. Then, our pretty newe come man will looke to be one.

 Truapenie. We foure I trust shall be a jolly mery knot.

Shall we sing a fitte[126] to welcome our friende, Annot?

 An. Alyface. Perchaune, he can not sing.

 D. Dough. I am at all assayes.

 Tib. Talk. By Cooke, and the better welcome to us alwayes.

Here they sing.

A thing very fitte

For them that have witte,

---

[126] *Sing a fitte.*] A *fit* is a song or glee.

166

And are felowes knitte,
Servants in sone house to bee;
As fast for to sitte,
And not oft to flitte,
Nor varie a whitte,
But lovingly to agree.

No man complainyng,
Nor other disdayning,
For losse or for gainyng,
But felowes or friends to bee;
No grudge remainyng,
No worke refrainyng,
Nor helpe restrainyng,
But lovingly to agree.

No man for despite,
By worde or by write,
His felowe to twite,
But further in honestie;
No good turnes entwite,
Nor olde sores recite,
But let all goe quite,
And lovingly to agree.

After drudgerie,
When they be werie,
Then to be merie,
To laugh and sing they be free;
With chip and cherie,
Heigh derie derie,
Trill on the berie,
And lovingly to agree.

Tib. Talk. Wyll you now in with us unto our mistresse go?
D. Dough. I have first for my maister an errand or two.

But, I have here from him a token and a ring;
They shall have moste thanke of hir, that first doth it bring.
   Tib. Talk. Mary, that will I.
   Trupenie. See, and Tibet snatch not now.
   Tib. Talk. And, why may not I, sir, get thanks as well as you?

                                    (Exeat.)

   An. Alyface. Yet, get ye not all, we will go with you both,
And have part of your thanks, be ye never so loth.

                            [Exeant Trupenie and Annot.
   D. Dough. So my handes are ridde of it, I care for no more.
I may now returne home: so durst I not afore.   *[Exeat.*

ACTUS ij.   SCÆNA iiij.

C. CUSTANCE — TIBET — ANNOT ALYFACE — TRUEPENIE.

   C. Custance. Nay, come forth all three: and come hither, pretie mayde;
Will not so many forewarnings make you afrayde?
   Tib. Talk. Yes, forsoth.
   C. Custance. But, stil be a runner up and downe?
Still be a bringer of tidings and tokens to towne?
   Tib. Talk. No, forsooth, mistresse.
   C. Custance. Is all your delite and joy
In whiskyng and ramping abroade, like a Tom boy?
   Tib. Talk. Forsoth, these were there too, Annot and Trupenie.
   Trupenie. Yea, but ye alone tooke it, ye can not denie.
   An Alyface. Yea, that ye did.
   Tib. Talk. But, if I had not, ye twaine would.
   C. Custance. You great calfe, ye shoulde have more witte, so ye should.
But, why shoulde any of you take such things in hande?
   Tib. Talk. Bicause it came from him that must be your husbande.
   C. Custance. How do ye know that?
   Tib. Talk. Forsoth, the boy did say so.
   C. Custance. What was his name?
   An. Alyface. We asked not.

C. Custance. Did [ye][127] no.?

An. Alyface. He is not farre gone, of likelyhood.

Trupenie. I will see.

C. Custance. If thou canst finde him in the streete, bring him to me.

Trupenie. Yes.   [*Exeat*.

C. Custance. Well, ye naughtie girles, if ever I pereeive

That henceforth you do letters or tokens receive,

To bring unto me, from any person or place,

Except ye first shewe me the partie face to face,

Eyther thou or then, fall truly abye[128] thou shalt.

   Tib. Talk. Pardon this, and the next time ponder me in salte.

   C. Custance. I shall make all girles, by you twaine, to beware.

   Tib. Talk. If I ever offende againe, do not me spare.

But, if ever I see that false boy any more,

By your mistreshyp's license, I tell you afore,

I will rather have my cote twentie times swinged,

Than on the naughtie wag not to be avenged.

   C. Custance. Good wenches would not so rampe abroade, ydelly,

But, keepe within doores, and plie their worke earnestly.

If one would speake with me, that is a man likely,

Ye shall have right good thanke to bring me word quickly;

But, otherwyse, with messages to come in post,

From henceforth, I promise you, shall be to your cost.

Get you in to your work.

   Tib. and Annot. Yes, forsooth.

   C. Custance. Hence, both twaine.

And let me see you play me such a part againe.

                                        [*Ex. Tib. and Annot*.

Re-enter TRUPENIE.

---

[127] The word within brackets is added.

[128] *Full truly abye thou shalt*.] To aby, means to rue, or suffer for. So in "The Midsummer Night's Dream," Act 3, Scene 2:—

> "Disparage not the faith thou dost not know,
> "Lest, to thy peril, thou *aby* it dear."

Trupenie. Maistresse, I have runne past the farre ende of the streete,
Yet, can I not yonder craftie boy see nor meete;
   C. Custance. No?
   Trupenie. Yet I looked as farre beyonde the people,
As one may see out of the toppe of Paula's steeple.
   C. Custance. Hence in at doores, and let me no more be vext!
   Trupenie. Forgeve me this one fault, and lay on for the next.   [*Exeat.*
   C. Custance. Now will I in too, for I thinke, so God me mende,
This will prove some foolishe matter the ende.   [*Exeat.*

ACTUS iij.   SCÆNA j.

MATHEWE MERYGREEKR.

   M. Mery. Nowe say [I] this againe: he hath somewhat to dooing
Which followeth the trace of one that is wowing;
Specially that hath no more witte in his hedde,
Than my cousin Roister Doister withall is ledde.
I am sent in all haste to espie and to marke
How our letters and tokens are likely to warke.
Maister Roister Doister must have answere in haste,
For, he loveth not to spends much labour in waste.
Nowe, as for Christian Custance, by this light,
Though she had not hir trouth to Gawin Goodluck plight,
Yet, rather than with such a loutishe dolte to marie,
I dare say she woulde lyve a poore lyfe solitarie.
But, faine woulda I speake with Custance, if I wist how,
To laugh at the matter. Yond' commeth one forth now.

ACTUS iij.   SCÆNA ij.

TIBET — M. MERYGREEKE.

   Tib. Talk. Ah! that I might but once in my life have a sight
Of him who made us all so yll shent; by this light,

He shoulde never escape, if I had him by the eare,

But, even from his head, I woulde it bite or teare.

Yea, and if one of them were not inowe,

I would bite them both off, I make God a vow.

  M. Mery. What is he, whom this little mouse doth so threaten?

  Tib. Talk. I woulde teache him, I trow, to make girles shent or beaten.

  M. Mery. I will call hir.—Maids, with whome are ye so hastie?

  Tib. Talk. Not with you, Sir, but with a little wagpastie;

A deceiver of folkes, by subtill craft and guile.

  M. Mery. (Aside.) I knowe where she is: Dobinet hath wrought some wile.

  Tib. Talk. He brought a ring and token, which he sayd was sent

From our dame's husbande, but I wot well I was shent:

For, it liked hir as well (to tell you no lies,)

As water in her shyppe, or salt cast in her eies:

And yet, whence it came, neyther we nor she can tell.

  M. Mery. We shall have sport anone:—I like this very walk.—*(Aside.)*

And, dwell ye here with mistresse Custance, faire maide?

  Tib. Talk. Yea, mary do I sir: what would ye have sayd?

  M. Mery. A little message unto hir, by worde of mouth.

  Tib. Talk. No messages, by your leave, nor tokens, forsooth.

  M. Mery. Then, helpe me to spake with hir.

  Tib. Talk. With a good will that.

Here she commeth forth. Now, speake; ye know best, what.

Enter C. CUSTANCE.

C. Custance. None other life with you, maide, but abrode to skip?

Tib. Talk. Forsooth, here is one would speake with your mistresship.

C. Custance. Ah, have ye ben learning of mo messages now?

Tib. Talk. I would not heare his minde, but had him shewe it to you.

C. Custance. In at dores!

Tib. Talk. I am gon.   *[Ex.*

M. Mery. Dame Custance, God ye save.

C. Custance. Welcome, friend Merygreeke: and, what thing wold ye have?

M. Mery. I am come to you, a little matter to breake.

C. Custance. But see it be honest, else better not to speake.

M. Mery. Howe feele ye yourselfe affected here of late?

C. Custance. I feele no maner change; but, after the olde rate.
But, whereby do ye meane?

M. Mery. Concerning mariage.
Doth not love lade you?

C. Custance. I feele no such cariage.

M. Mery. Doe ye feele no pangues of dotage? Aunswere me right.

C. Custance. I dote so, that I make but one sleeps all the night.
But, what neede all these wordes?

M. Mery. Oh, Jesus! will ye see
What dissemblyng creatures these same women be?
The gentleman ye wote of, whome ye doe so love
That ye woulda faine marrie him, yf ye durst it move,
(Among other riche widowes, which are of him glad,)
Lest ye for lesing of him perchaunce might runne mad,
Is nowe contented that, upon your sute making,
Ye be as one in election of taking.

C. Custance. What a tale is this!—That I wote of! Whome I love!

M. Mery. Yea, and he is as loving a worme again as a dove.
E'en of very pitie he is willyng you to take,
Bicause ye shall not destroy your selfe for his sake.

C. Custance. Mary, God yelde his maship, what ever he be,
It is gentlemanly spoken.

M. Mery. Is it not trow ye?
If ye have the grace now to offer your selfe, ye speede.

C. Custance. As muche as though I did; this time it shall not neede.
But, what gentleman is it, I pray you tell me plaine,
That woweth so finely?

M. Mery. Lo where ye be againe
As though ye knewe him not.

C. Custance. Tush! ye speake in jest.

M. Mery. Nay, sure the partie is in good knacking earnest,
And have you he will (he sayth) and have you he must.

C. Custance. I am promised duryng my lyfe; that is just.

M. Mery. Mary, so thinketh he, unto him alone.

C. Custance. No creature hath my faith and trouth but one,
That is Gawin Goodlucke: and if it be not hee,
He hath no title this way, what ever he be,
For, I knowe none to whome I have such worde spoken.

    M. Mery. Ye knowe him not you, by his letter and token?

    C. Custance. Indede true it is, that a letter I have,
But I never reade it yet, as God [shall] me save.

    M. Mery. Ye a woman? and your letter so long unredde.

    C. Custance. Ye may thereby know what hast I have to wedde.
But now, who it is for my hande, I knowe by gesse.

    M. Mery. Ah! well, I say.

    C. Custance. It is Roister Doister, doubtlesse.

    M. Mery. Will ye never leave this dissimulation?
Ye know hym not?

    C. Custance. But by imagination;
For, no man there is but a very dolte and loute
That to wowe a widowe woulde so go about.
He shall never have me his wife while he doe live.

    M. Mery. Then will he have you if he may, so mote I thrive;
And he biddeth you sende him worde by me,
That ye humbly beseech him ye may his wife be,
And that there shall be no let in you, nor mistrust,
But to be wedded on Sunday next if he lust;
And biddeth you to looke for him.

    C. Custance. Doth he byd so?

    M. Mery. When he commeth, aske hym whether he dyd or no?

    C. Custance. Goe say, that I bid him keepe him warme at home,
For, if he come abroade, he shall cough me a mome.[129]
My mynde was vexed, I 'shrew his head, sottish dolt.

    M. Mery. He hath in his head—

---

[129] *A mome.*] A mome is a blockhead. See Act 5, Scenes 2 and 5. A passage similar to that in the text, occurs in Lilly's "Mother Bombie," 1594:—"I know he will cough for anger that I yield not; but, he shall *cough me* a fool for his labour."

C. Custance. As much braine as a burbolt.[130]

M. Mery. Well, dame Custance, if he heare you thus play choploge.

C. Custance. What will he?

M. Mery. Play the devill in the horologe.

C. Custance. I defye him, loute.

M. Mery. Shall I tell hym what ye say?

C. Custance. Yea, and adde what so ever thou canst, I thee pray,
And I will a vouche it what so ever it bee.

M. Mery. Then let me alone; we will laugh well, ye shall see;
It will not be long ere he will hither resorte.

C. Custance. Let hym come when hym lust, I wishe no better sporte.
Fare ye well, I will in, and read my great letter:
I shall to my wower make answere the better.   [*Excat.*

ACTUS iij.   SCÆNA iij.

MATHEW MERYGREEKE — ROISTER DOISTER.

M. Mery. Now that the whole answere in my devise doth rest,
I shall paint out our wower in colours of the best,
And all that I say shall be on Custance's mouth,
She is author of all that I shall speake forsoth.
But, yond commeth Roister Doister nowe, in a traunce.

R. Royster. Juno sende me this day good lucke and good chaunce.
I can not but come see howe Merygreeke doth speede.

M. Mery. I will not see him, but give him a jutte[131] in deede.
I crie your mastershyp mercie!

R. Royster. And whither now?

M. Mery. As fast as I could runne, sir, in poste against you.

---

[130] *A burbolt.*] i. e. a birdbolt, a short thick arrow, with a blunt head, made use of to kill rooks. It appears to have been looked upon as an emblem of dulness. So in Marston's "What You Will," 1607,

> "Ignorance should shoot
His gross-knobb'd *bird-bolt*."

[131] *A jutte.*] i. e. a jostle.

But, why speake ye so faintly, or why are ye so sad?

    R. Royster. Thou knowest the proverb,—bycause I can not be had.
Hast thou spoken with this woman?

    M. Mery. Yea, that I have.

    R. Royster. And what, will this geare be?

    M. Mery. No, so God me save.

    R. Royster. Hast thou a flat answer?

    M. Mery. Nay, a sharp answer.

    R. Royster. What?

    M. Mery. Ye shall not, (she sayth) by hir will, marry hir cat.
Ye are suche a calfe, such an asse, suche a blocke,
Such a lilburne, such a hoball, such a lobcocke;
And, bicause ye shoulde come to hir at no season,
She despised your maship out of all reason.
"Beware what ye say (ko I) of such a jentman!"
"Nay, I feare him not (ko she) doe the best he can."
He vaunteth him selfe for a man of prowesse greate,
Whereas, a good gander, I dare say, may him beate.
And whereas he is louted[132] and laughed to scorne,
For the veriest dolte that ever was borne;
And veriest lubber, sloven and beast,
Living in this worlde, from the west to the east:
Yet, of himselfe hath he suche opinion,
That in all the worlde is not like the minion.
He thinketh eche woman to be brought in dotage,
With the onely sight of his goodly personage:
Yet, none that will have hym: we do hym loute and flocke,
And make him among us, our common sporting stocke;
And so would I now (ko she) save onely bicause,—
("Better nay," ko I)—"I lust not medle with dawes."

---

    [132] *Louted.*] i. e. mocked or despised. The word is used by *York* in the "First Part of Henry
6th," Act 4, Scene 3.

               "I am *lowted* by a traitor villain."

    On this simple passage, the commentators have written half-a-dozen learned Notes, and
have mistaken its meaning after all. *Lout* and *Flout* are synonimous.

"Ye are happy (ko I) that ye are a woman,
This would cost you your life in case ye were a man."
    R. Royster. Yea, an hundred thousand pound should not save hir life.
    M. Mery. No, but that ye wowe hir to have hir to your wife;
But I coulde not stoppe hir mouth.
    R. Royster. Heigh how, alas!
    M. Mery. Be of good cheere man, and let the worlde passe.[133]
    R. Royster. What shall I doe or say, nowe that it will not bee?
    M. Mery. Ye shall have choise of a thousand as good as shee;
And ye must pardon hir; it is for lacke of witte.
    R. Royster. Yea, for were not I an husbande for hir fitte?
Well, what should I now doe?
    M. Mery. In faith I can not tell.
    R. Royster. I will go home and die.
    M. Mery. Then, shall I bidde toll the bell?
    R. Royster. No.
    M. Mery. God have mercie on your soule, ah good gentleman,
That er ye shoulde thus dye for an unkinde woman.
Will ye drinke once ere ye goe?
    R. Royster. No, No, I will none.
    M. Mery. How feele your soule to God?
    R. Royster. I am nigh gone.
    M. Mery. And shall we hence streight?
    R. Royster. Yea.
    M. Mery. Placebo dilexi.   [*ut infra.*[134]
Maister Roister Doister will streight go home and die.
    R. Royster. Heigh how! alas! the pangs of death my hearte do breake.
    M. Mery. Holde your peace, for shame, sir! a dead man may not speake.
    Nequando: What mourners and what torches shall we have?
    R. Royster. None.
    M. Mery. Dirige. He will go darklyng to his grave,—
Neque lux, neque crux, neque mourners, *neque* clinke,

---

[133] A proverbial expression of heedless jollity. See the Induction to the "Taming of the Shrew," where *Sly* exclaims:—"Paucas pallabris; *let the world slide*: Sessa!"

[134] See the end of the Comedy.

He will steale to heaven, unknowing to God, I thinke;
A porta inferi; who shall your goodes possesse?
    R. Royster. Thou shalt be my sectour, and have all, more and lesse.
    M. Mery. Requiem æternam. Now, God reward your mastershyp,
And I will crie halfepenie doale for your worshyp.
Come forth, Sirs; heare the doleful newes I shall you tell.

[Evocat servos milites.

Our good maister here will no longer with us dwell,
But, in spite of Custance, which hath hym weried,
Let us see his mashyp solemnely buried;
And while some piece of his soule is yet hym within,
Some part of his funeralls let us here begin.
Audivi vocem. All men take head by this one gentleman,
How you sette your love upon an unkinde woman.
For, these women be all such madde, pievish elves,
They will not be wonne, except it please them selves.
But, in fayth, Custance, if ever ye come in hell,
Maister Roister Doister shall serve you as well.
And will ye needes go from us thus in very deede?
    R. Royster. Yea, in good sadnesse.
    M. Mery. Now, Jesus Christ be your speede.
Good night, Roger olde knave! farewell Roger olde knave!
Good night, Roger olde knave, knave knap!   [*ut infra.*[135]
Pray for the late maister Roister Doister's soule,
And come forth, parish clarke; let the passing-bell toll.

[Ad servos milites.

Pray for your mayster, Sirs; and for hym ring a peale.
He was your right good maister while he was in heale.
    R. Royster. Qui Lazarum.
Heigh how.
    M. Mery. Dead men go not so fast.
    R. Royster. In Paradisum.
Heihow.

---

[135] See the end of the Comedy.

M. Mery. Soft, heare what I have cast.

R. Royster. I will heare nothing, I am past.

M. Mery. Whough, well away.

Ye may tarie one houre, and heare what I shall say.

Ye were best, Sir, for a while to revive againe,

And quite them er ye go.

R. Royster. Trowest thou so?

M. Mery. Yea, plain.

R. Royster. How may I revive, being new so farre past?

M. Mery. I will rubbe your temples, and fette you againe at last.

R. Royster. It will not be possible.

M. Mery. Yes for twentie pounde.

R. Royster. Armes! what dost thou?

M. Mery. Fet you again out of your swound.

By this crosse, ye were nigh gone in deede; I might feele

Your soule departing within an inch of your heele.

Now, folow my counsell.

R. Royster. What is it?

M. Mery. If I wer you,

Custance shoulde eft seeke to me, ere I woulde bowe.

R. Royster. Well, as thou wilt have me, even so will I doe.

M. Mery. Then, shall ye revive againe for an hour or two.

R. Royster. As thou wilt: I am content, for a little space.

M. Mery. Good happe is not hastie: yet in space comth grace.

To speake with Custance your selfe, shoulde be very well;

What good thereof may come, nor I, nor you can tell.

But, now the matter standeth upon your mariage,

Ye must now take unto you a lustie courage.

Ye may not speake with a faint heart to Custance,

But with a lusty breast and countenance,

That she may knowe she hath to answere to a man.

R. Royster. Yes, I can do that as well as any can.

M. Mery. Then, bicause ye must Custance face to face wowe,

Let us see how to behave your self ye can doe.

Ye must have a portely bragge after your estate.

R. Royster. Tushe, I can handle that after the best rate.

M. Mery. Well done; so loe! up man, with your head and chin;

Up with that snoute man: so loe, nowe ye begin.

So, that is somewhat like; but prankie cote, nay whan,

That is a lustie brute; handes under your side, man:

So loe; now is it even as it shoulde bee;

That is somewhat like, for a man of your degree.

Then must ye stately goe, jetting up and downe.

Tut, can ye no better shake the taile of your gowne?

There loe, such a lustie bragge it is ye must make.

    R. Royster. To come behind, and make curtsie,[136] thou must some pains
        take.

    M. Mery. Else were I much to blame. I thanke your mastership;

The Lorde one day all to begrime you with worshyp.

Backe, Sir sauce! let gentlefolkes have elbow roome!

Voyde Sirs, see ye not Maister Roister Deister come?

Make place, my maisters.

    R. Royster. Thou justlest nowe to nigh.

    M. Mery. Backe, al rude loutes.

    R. Royster. Tush.

    M. Mery. I crie your maship mercy.

Hoighdagh, if faire fine Mistresse Custance sawe you now,

Ralph Roister Doister were hir owne I warrant you.

    R. Royster. Neare an M. by your girdle?

    M. Mery. Your good Mastershypp's

Maistershyp, were hir owne mistreshyp's mistreshyp's.

Ye were take up for haukes; ye were gone, ye were gone:

But, now one other thing more yet I thinke upon.

    R. Royster. Shewe what it is.

    M. Mery. A wower, be he never so poore,

Must play and sing before his best belove's doore.

How much more then you?

    R. Royster. Thou speakest wel out of dout.

---

[136] *Curtsie.*] This word was formerly applied to any kind of obeisance, either of man or woman.

M. Mery. And perchaunce that would make hir the sooner come out.

R. Royster. Goe call my musitians, bydde them high apace.

M. Mery. I wyll be here with them, ere ye can say trey ace.   [*Exeat.*

R. Royster. This was well sayde of Merygreeke, I loue his wit,

Before my sweete heart's dore wee will have a fit.

That if my love come forth, I may with hir talke;

I doubt not but this geare shall on my side walke.

But lo, how well Merygreeke is returned sence.

Re-enter M. MERYGREEKE.

M. Mery. There hath grown no grasse on my heele since I went
    hence;—

Lo here have I brought that shall make you pastance.

R. Royster. Come, sirs, let us sing, to winne my deare love Custance.
          [*Cantent.*[137]

M. Mery. Lo, where she commeth; some countenance to hir make;

And ye shall heare me be plaine with hir for your sake.

ACTUS iij.   SCÆNA iiij.

CUSTANCE — MERYGREEKE — ROISTER DOISTER.

C. Custance. What gaudyng and foolyng is this afore my doore?

M. Mery. May not folks be honest, pray you, though they be poore?

C. Custance. As that thing may be true, so rich folkes may be fooles.

R. Royster. (*to M. Mery.*) Hir talke is as fine as she had learned in schooles.

M. Mery. (*to R. Royster.*) Looke partly towarde hir, and draw a little nere.

C. Custance. Get ye home, idle folkes.

M. Mery. Why may not we be here?

Nay and ye will haze, haze;[138] otherwise, I tell you plaine,

And ye will not haze, then give us our geare againe.

C. Custance. In deede, I have of yours much gay things God save all.

---

[137] See the end of the Comedy.

[138] *i. e.* If you will have us, have us.

R. Royster. (*to M. Mery.*) Speake gently unto hir, and let her take all.

M. Mery. (*to R. Royster.*) Ye are too tender hearted:

  Shall she make us dawes!—

Nay, dame, I will be plaine with you m my friend's cause.

 R. Royster. Let all this passe, sweet heart, and accept my service.

 C. Custance. I will not be served with a foole, in no wise.

When I choose an husbande, I hope to take a man.

 M. Mery. And, where will ye finde one which can doe that he can?

Now, thys man towarde you being so kinde,

Why not make him an answere somewhat to his mind?

 C. Custance. I sent him a full answere by you, dyd I not?

 M. Mery. And I reported it.

 C. Custance. Nay, I must speake it againe.

 R. Royster. No, no, he tolde it all.

 M. Mery. Was I not metely plaine?

 R. Royster. Yes.

 M. Mery. But, I would not tell all; for, faith if I had,

With you, dame Custance, are this houre, it had ben bad;

And, not without cause: for, this goodly personage,

Ment no lesse than to joyne with you in mariage.

 C. Custance. Let him wast no more labour nor sute about me.

 M. Mery. Ye know not where your preferment lieth I see;—

He sendeth you such a token, ring, and letter.

 C. Custance. Mary, heye it is; ye never sawe a better.

 M. Mery. Let us see your letter.

 C. Custance. Holde! reade it if ye can;

And see what letter it is to winne a woman.

 M. Mery.

To myne owne deare coney birde, sweete heart, and pigsny,

 Good Mistresse Custance, present these by and by.

Of this superscription do ye blame the stile?

 C. Custance. With the rest, as good stuffe as ye redde a great while.

 M. Mery.

Sweete Mistresse, where as I love you nothing at all,
Regarding your substance and richesse chiefe of all;
For your personage, beautie, demeanour, and wit,
I commende me unto you never a whit.
Sorie to heare report of your good welfare,
For, (as I heare say) suche youre conditions are,
That ye be worthie favour of no living man;
To be abhorred of every honest man.
To be taken for a woman enclined to vice;
Nothing at all to vertue gyving hir due price.
Wherefore, concerning mariage, ye are thought
Such a fine paragon as nere honest man bought.
And nowe, by these presentes, I do you advertise
That I am minded to marrie you in no wise.
For your goodes and substance, I could bee content
To take you as ye are. If ye mynde to be my wyfe,
Ye shall be assured for the tyme of my lyfe
I will keepe ye ryght well from good rayment and fare;—
Ye shall not be kepte but in sorrowe and care.
Ye shall in no wyse lyve at your owne libertie;
Doe and say what ye lust, ye shall never please me;
But when ye are merie, I will be all sadde;
When ye are sorie, I will be very gladde;
When ye seeke your hearte's ease, I will be unkinde;
At no tyme in me shall ye muche gentlenesse finde;
But, all things contrary to your will and minde
Shall be done: otherwise I will not be behinde
To speake. And all them that would do you wrong,
I will so helpe and mainteyne, ye shall not lyve long.
Nor any foolishe dolta shall cumbre you, but I;
I, who ere say nay, wyll sticke by you tyll I die.
Thus, good Mistresse Custance, the Lorde you save and keepe
From me, Roister Doister, whether I wake or slepe.
Who favoureth you no lesse (ye may be bolde)[139]
Than this letter purporteth, which ye have unfolde.

---

[139] *Be bolde.*] i. e. be assured. So in Act 3, Scene 2:—
      "I will be even with thee, thou beast, *thou may be bolde.*"

C. Custance. Howe, by this letter of love? is it not fine?

R. Royster. By the Armes of Caleys, it is none of myne.

M. Mery. Fie! you are fowle to blame; this is your owne hand.

C. Custance. Might not a woman he proude of such an husbande?

M. Mery. Ah, that ye would in a letter shew such despite!

R. Royster. Oh, I would had hym here, the which did it endite!

M. Mery. Why, ye made it your selfe, ye tolde me, by this light!

R. Royster. Yea, I ment I wrote it myne owhe selfe yesternight.

C. Custance. Y'wis, Sir, I would not have sent you such a mocke.

R. Royster. Ye may so take it; but, I ment it not so, by Cocke.

M. Mery. Who can blame this woman, to fume, and fret, and rage?
Tut, tut, your owne selfe nowe have marde your marriage.
Well, yet, Mistresse Custance, if ye can, this remitte;
This gentleman otherwise may your love requitte.

C. Custance. So, God be with you both, and seeke no more to me.

[Exeat.

R. Royster. Wough, she is gone for ever, I shall hir no more see.

M. Mery. What weepe? Fye for shame! And blubber?
For manhod's sake,
Never lette your foe so muche pleasure of you take.
Rather play the man's parte, and doe [from] love refraine
If she despise you, e'en despise ye hir againe.

R. Royster. By Gosse, and for thy sake, I defye hir in deede!

M. Mery. Yea, and perchaunce that way ye shall much sooner speede;
For, one madde propretie these women have in fey,[140]
When ye will, they will not: will not ye? then will they.
Ah, foolishe woman! ah, moste unluckie Custance!
Ah, unfortunate woman! ah, pievishe Custance,
Art thou to thy harmes so obstinately bent,
That thou canst not see where lieth thine high preferment?
Canst thou not lub dis man, which coulde lub dee so well?
Art thou so much thine owne foe?

R. Royster. Thou dost the truth tell.

---

[140] *In fey.*] i. e. in faith: from the French, *foy.*

M. Mery. Well, I lament.

R. Royster. So do I.

M. Mery. Wherfor?

R. Royster. For this thing,

Bicause she is gone.

M. Mery. I mourne for an other thing.

R. Royster. What is it, Merygreeke, wherfore thou dost griefe take?

M. Mery. That I am not a woman myselfe, for your sake.

I would have you myselfe, and a strawe for yond' gill,

And make much of you, though it were against my will.

I would not, I warrant you, fall in such a rage,

As to refuse suche a goodly personage.

R. Royster. In faith, I heartily thanke thee, Merygreeke.

M. Mery. And were I a woman——

R. Royster. Thou wouldest to me seeke.

M. Mery. For, though I say it, a goodly person ye bee;

R. Royster. No, No.

M. Mery. Yes, a goodly man as e're I dyd see.

R. Royster. No, I am a poore homely man, as God made mee.

M. Mery. By the faith that I owe to God, sir, but ye bee.

Woulde I might, for your sake, spende a thousande pound land.

R. Royster. I dare say thou wouldest have me to thy husbande.

M. Mery. Yea, and I were the fairest lady in the shiere,

And knewe you as I know you, and see you nowe here.

Well, I say no more.

R. Royster. Gramercies, with all my hart.

M. Mery. But, since that can not be, will ye play a wyse parte?

R. Royster. How should I?

M. Mery. Refraine from Custance a while now,

And I warrant hir soone right glad to seeke to you.

Ye shall see hir anon come on hir knees creeping,

And pray you to be good to hir, salte teares weeping.

R. Royster. But what, and she come not?

M. Mery. In faith, then, farewel she.

Or else, if ye be wroth, ye may avenged be.

R. Royster. By Cooke's precious potsticke, and e'en so I shall;
I wyll utterly destroy hir, and house and all.
But, I woulde be avenged in the meane space,
On that vile scribler, that did my wowing disgrace.

M. Mery. Scribler ko you? In deede, he is worthy no lesse.
I will call hym to you, and ye bidde me, doubtlesse.

R. Royster. Yes, for although he had as many lives
As a thousande widowes, and'a thousande wives,
As a thousande lyons, and a thousande rattes,
A thousande wolves, and a thousande cattes,
A thousand bulles, and a thousande calves,
And a thousande legions divided in halves,
He shall never scape death on my sworde's point,
Though I shoulde be torne therfore joynt by joynt.

M. Mery. Nay, if ye will kyll him, I will not fette him,
I will not in so much extremitie sette him.
He may yet amende, Sir, and be an honest man;
Therfore, pardon him, good soule, as muche as ye can.

R. Royster. Well, for thy sake, this once, with his lyfe he shall passe;
But, I wyll hewe hym all to pieces, by the masse.

M. Mery. Nay, fayth, ye shall promise that he shall no harm have,
Else I will not fet him.

R. Royster. I shall, so God me save!
But I may chide him a-good.[141]

M. Mery. Yea, that do hardely.

R. Royster. Go then.

M. Mery. I returne, and bring him to you, by and by.[142]

[*Ex.*

---

[141] *A good.*] In earnest—heartily. So in Marlowe's "Jew of Malta," 1633, Act 2, Scene 3:—
——"I have laugh'd *a-good* to see the cripples
"Go limping home to Christendom on stilts."
[142] *By and by.*] This expression, though now used to denote some little lapse of time, formerly signified *immediately*. It occurs again, in the same sense, more than once in this play.

<h1 style="text-align:center">ACTUS iij.   SCÆNA v.</h1>

ROYSTER DOISTER — MATHEW MERYGREEKE — SCRIVENER.

R. Royster. What is a gentleman, but his worde and his promise?
I must now save this vilaine's lyfe, in any wise;
And yet, at hym already my handes doe tickle,
I shall uneth[143] holde them, they will be so fickle.
But lo, and Merygreeke have not brought him sens![144]
 M. Mery. Nay, I woulde I had of my purse payde fortie pens.
 Scrivener. So woulde I too: but, it needed not that stounde.[145]
 M. Mery. But, the jentman had rather spent five thousande pounde;
For, it disgraced him at least five tymes so muche.
 Scrivener. He disgraced hym selfe, his loutishnesse is suche.
 R. Royster. Howe long they stande prating! Why com'st thou not away?
 M. Mery. Come nowe to hymselfe, and hearke what he will say.
 Scrivener. I am not afrayde in his presence to appeere.
 R. Royster. Art thou come felow?
 Scrivener. How thinke you? Am I not here?
 R. Royster. What hindrance hast thou done me, and what villanie!
 Scrivener. It hath come of thy selfe, if thou hast had any.
 R. Royster. All the stocke thou comest of, later or rather,[146]
From thy fyrst father's grandfather's father's father,
Nor all that shall come of thee, to the worlde's ende,
Though to three score generations they descende,
Can be able to make a just recompence,
For this trespasse of thine, and this one offense.
 Scrivener. Wherin?
 R. Royster. Did not you make me a letter, brother?

---

 [143] *Uneth.*] With difficulty—scarcely. So in Act 2, Scene 4, of the "Second Part of Henry the Sixth:"—

<blockquote>"*Uneath* may she endure the flinty streets."</blockquote>

 [144] *Sens*] Already.

 [145] *Stounde.*] This word is put by Spenser for a tumult or bustle, in which sense it appears to be used in the text.

 [146] *Rather.*] i. e. earlier. *Rath,* for early, occurs in Chaucer.

186

Scrivener. Pay the like hire, I will make you suche an other.

R. Royster. Nay! see, and these whoreson Phariseys and Scribes
Doe not get their living by polling[147] and bribes.
If it were not for shame——

Scrivener. Nay, holde thy handes still.[148]

M. Mery. Why, did ye not promise that ye would not him spill?[149]

Scrivener. Let him not spare me.

R. Royster. Why, wilt thou strike me again?

Scrivener. Ye shall have as good as ye bring of me, that is plaine.

M. Mery. I cannot blame him, sir, though your blowes wold him greve;
For he knoweth present death to ensue of all ye geve.

R. Royster. Well, this man for once hath purchased thy pardon.

Scrivener. And now, what say ye to me? or else I will be gon.

R. Royster. I say, the letter thou madest me, was not good.

Scrivener. Then did ye wrong copy it, of likelyhood.

R. Royster. Yes, out of thy copy, worde for worde, I it wrote.

Scrivener. Then, was it as you prayed to have it, I wote;
But, in reading and pointyng, there was made some faulte.

R. Royster. I wote not; but, it made all my matter to haulte.

Scrivener. Howe say you, is this mine originall or no?

R. Royster. The selfe same that I wrote out of, so mote I go.

Scrivener. Loke you on your owne fist, and I will looke on this,
And let this man be judge whether I reade amisse.

> To myne owne deare coney birde, sweete heart, and piysny,
> Good Mistresse Custance, present thee by and by.

How now? doth, not this superscription agree?

R. Royster. Reade that is within, and there ye shall the fault see.

----

[147] *Polliny.*] i. e. plundering:
> "Which *polls* and pills the poor in piteous wise."
> "*Faerie Queen*," Book 5, Canto 2.

[148] From the *Scrivener's* next speech, it seems as if this hemistic ought to be given to *Merygreeke.*

[149] *Spill.*] i. e. destroy. So *Lear,*
> ——"All germens *spill* at once,
> "That make ingrateful man." Act 3, Scene 2.

Sweete Mistresse, where as I love you; nothing at all
Regarding your substance and richesse; chiefe of all
For your personage, beautie, demeanour, and wit,
I commende me unto you; never a whit
Sorie to heare report of your good welfare;
For, (as I heare say) suche youre conditions are,
That ye be worthie favour; of no living man
To be abhorred; of every honest man
To be taken for a woman enclined to vice
Nothing at all; to vertue gyving hir due price.
Wherefore, concerning mariage, ye are thought
Such a fine paragon as ne're honest man bought.
And nowe, by these presentes, I do you advertise
That I am minded to marrie you; in no wise
For your goodes and substance; I could bee content
To take you as ye are; If ye mynde to be my wyfe,
Ye shall be assured for the tyme of my lyfe,
I will keepe ye ryght well: from good rayment and fare
Ye shall not be kepte: but, in sorrowe and care
Ye shall in no wyse lyve; at your owne libertie,
Doe and say what ye lust; ye shall never please me
But when ye are merie; I will be all sadde
When ye are sorie; I will be very gladde
When ye seeke your hearte's ease; I will be unkinde
At no tyme; in me shall ye muche gentlenesse finde.
But, all things contrary to your will and minde
Shall be done otherwise. I will not be behinde
To speake; and all them that would do you wrong
(I will so helpe and mainteyne ye) shall not lyve long.
Nor any foolishe dolte shall cumbre you; but I,
I, who are say nay, wyll sticke by you tyll I die.
Thus, good Mistresse Custance, the Lorde you save and keepe!
From me; Roister Doister, whether I wake or slepe,
Who favoureth you no lesse (ye may be holde)

Than this letter purporteth which ye have unfolde.[150]

Now Sir, what default can ye finde in this letter?

   R. Royster. Of truth, in my mynde, there can not be a better.

   Scrivener. Then was the fault in readyng, and not in writyng,

No, nor I dare say, in the fourme of endityng.

But, who read this letter, that it sounded so nought?

   M. Mery. I redde it in deede.

   Scrivener. Ye red it not as ye ought.

   R. Royster. Why, thou wretched villaine, was all this same fault in thee?

   M. Mery. I knocke your costarde,[151] if ye offer to strike me.

   R. Royster. Strikest thou in deede, and I offer but in jest?

   M. Mery. Yea, and rappe ye againe, except ye can sit in rest.

And I will no longer tarie here, me beleve.

   R. Royster. What, wilt thou be angry, and I do thee forgave?

Fare thou well, scribler; I crie thee mercie in deede.

   Scrivener. Fare ye well, bibbler, and worthily may ye speede.

                                                   [Ex.

   R. Royster. If it were an other than thou, it were a knave.

   M. Mery. Ye are an other your selfe, sir, the Lorde us both save;

Albeit, in this matter I must your pardon crave.

Alas, woulde ye wyshe in me the witte that ye have?

But, as for my fault, I can quickely [it] amende:

I will shewe Custance it was I that did offende.

   R. Royster. By so doing, hir anger may be reformed.

   M. Mery. But, if by no entreatie she will be turned,

Then sette lyght by hir, and bee as testie as shee,

And doe your force upon hir with extremitie.

   R. Royster. Come on, therefore, lette us go home in sadnesse.

   M. Mery. That if force shall neede, all may be in a readinesse.

And as for thys letter, hardely let all go;

We wyll know whe're she refuse you for that or no.

                                              [Exeant. am.

---

[150] This is perhaps the earliest specimen of laborious ingenuity in the art of inditing equivocal epistles, which our language affords.

[151] *Costarde.*] Head.

<h2 style="text-align:center">ACTUS iiij.   SCÆNA j.</h2>

SYM. SURESBY.

Sym. Sure. Is there any man but I, Sym Suresby, alone,
That would have taken such an enterprise him upon;
In suche an outrageous tempest as this was,
Suche a daungerous gulfe of the sea to passe?
I thinke, verily, Neptune's mightie godshyp,
Was angry with some that was in our shyp,
And, but for the honestie which in me he founde,
I thinke for the others' sake we had bene drownde.
But, fye on that servant which for his maister's wealth[152]
Will sticke for to hazarde both his lyfe and his health.
My maister, Gawyn Goodlucke, after me a day,
Bicause of the weather, thought best his shyppe to stay;
And, now that I have the rough sourges so well past,
God graunt I may finde all things safe here at last:
Then will I thinke all my travaile well spent.
Nowe, the first poynt wherfore my maister hath me sent,
Is to salute dame Christian Custance, his wife
Espoused, whome he tendreth no lesse than his life.
I must see how it is with hir, well or wrong,
And whether for him she doth net now thinke long.
Then to other friendes I have a message or tway;
And then so to returne and mete him on the way.
Now wyll I goe knocke, that I may dispatche with speede;
But loe, forth commeth hir selfe happily in deede.

---

[152] *Wealth.*] Welfare or prosperity. Thus, in the *Litany* of the Church of England:—"In all time of our tribulation, in all time of our *wealth.*"

ACTUS iiij.   SCÆNA ij.

CHRISTIAN CUSTANCE — SYM. SURESBY.

C. Custance. I come to see if any more stirryng be here;
But, what straunger is this, which doth to me appere?
  Sym. Sure. I will speake to hir. Dame, the Lorde you save and see.
  C. Custance. What, friende Sym Suresby? Forsoth, right welcome ye be.
How doth mine owne Gawyn Goodlucke, I pray thee tell?
  Sym. Sure. When he knoweth of your health, he will be perfect well.
  C. Custance. If he have perfect helth, I am as I would be.
  Sym. Sure. Such newes will please him well. This is as it should be.
  C. Custance. I thinke now long for him.
  Sym. Sure. And he as long for you.
  C. Custance. When will he be at home?
  Sym. Sure. His heart is here e'en now;
His body commeth after.
  C. Custance. I woulde see that faine.
  Sym. Sure. As faste as wynde and sayle can cary it amaine.
But, what two men are yonde comming hitherwarde?
  C. Custance; Now, I'shrew their best Christmasse 'chekes, both
    togetherward!

ACTUS iiij.   SCÆNA iij.

CHRISTIAN CUSTANCE — SYM. SURESBY — RALPH ROYSTER
DOYSTER — MATHEW MERYGREEKE.

C. Custance. What meane these lawde felowes, thus to trouble me stil?
Sym Suresby here, perchaunce, shal thereof deme som yll;
And shall suspect in me some point of naughtinesse.
And they come hitherward.
  Sym. Sure. What is their businesse?

C. Custance. I have nought to them, nor they to me, in sadnesse.[153]

Sym. Sure. Let us hearken them; somewhat there is, I feare it.

R. Royster. I will speake out aloude best, that she may heare it.

M. Mery. Nay, alas, ye may so feare hir out of hir wit.

R. Royster. By the crosse of my sworde, I will hurt hir no whit.

M. Mery. Will ye doe no harme in deede? Shall I trust your worde?

R. Royster. By Roister Doister's fayth, I will speak but in borde[154]

Sym. Sure. Let us hearken them; somewhat there is, I feare it.

R. Royster. I will speake out aloude, I care not who heare it.—

Sirs, see that my harnesse, my tergat, and my shield,

Be made as bright now, as when I was last in fielde,

As white as I shoulde to warre agnine to morrowe:

For, sicke shall I be, but I worke some folke sorowe.

Therfore, see that all shine as bright as Sainct George,

Or as doth a key, newly come from the smith's forge.

I woulde have my sworde and harnesse to shine so bright,

That I might therwith dimme mine enemies' sight.

I would have it cast beames as fast, I tell you, playne,

As doth the glittryng grasse after a showre of raine.

And see that, in case I shoulde neede to come to arming,

All things may be ready at a minute's warning.

For, such chaunce may chaunce in an houre, do ye heare?

M. Mery. As perchance shall not chaunce againe in seven yeare.

R. Royster. Now, draw we neare to hir, and here what shall be sayde.

M. Mery. But, I woulde not have you make hir too muche afrayde.

R. Royster. Well founde, sweete wife, (I trust) for al this your soure looke.

C. Custance. Wife!—why cal ye me wife?

Sym. Sure. Wife!—This gear goeth acrook.

M. Mery. Nay, Mistresse Custance, I warrant you, our letter

Is not as we redde e'en nowe, but much better;

---

[153] *In sadnasse.*] In sooth—seriously.

[154] *In borde.*] Vide Note 106.

And, where ye halfe stomaked[155] this gentleman afore,
For this same letter, ye wyll love hym nowe therefore;
Nor, it is not this letter, though ye were a queene,
That shoulde breake marriage betweene you twaine, I weene.

    C. Custance. I did not refuse hym for the letter's sake;

    R. Royster. Then, ye are content me for your husbande to take.

    C. Custance. You for my husbande to take! Nothing lesse, truely.

    R. Royster. Yea, say so, sweete spouse; afore straungers hardly.

    M. Mery. And, though I have here his letter of love with me,
Yet, his ring and tokens he sent, keepe safe with ye.

    C. Custance. A mischiefe take his tokens, and him, and thee too!
But, what prate I with fooles? Have I nought else to doo?
Come in with me, Sym Suresby, to take some repast.

    Sym. Sure. I must, ere I drinke, by your leave, goe in all hast
To a place or two, with earnest letters of his.

    C. Custance. Then come drinke here with me.

    Sym. Sure. I thanke you.

    C. Custance. Do not misse.
You shall have a token to your maister with you;

    Sym. Sure. No tokens this time, gramercies.
God be with you.   *[Exeat.*

    C. Custance. Surely, this fellowe misdeemeth some yll in me;
Which thing, but God helpe, will go neere to spill me.[156]

    R. Royster. Yea, farewell fellow, and tell thy maister Goodlucke,
That he commeth to late of thys blossome to plucke.
Let him keepe him there still, or at leastwise make no hast;
As for his labour hither he shall spend in wast.
His betters be in place nowe.

    M. Mery. (*Aside.*) As long as it will hold.

---

[155] *Stomaked.*] To stomach is to dislike or resent. In "Antony and Cleopatra," Act iii.
Scene 4, *Octavia* says to *Antony*—
                        "O my good lord,
    "Believe not all; or, if you must believe,
    "*Stomach* not all."
[156] *Spill me.*] Vide Note 149.

C. Custance. I will be even with thee, thou beast, thou may be bolde.

R. Royster. Will ye have us then?

C. Custance. I will never have thee.

R. Royster. Then, will I have you?

C. Custance. No, the devill shal have thee.

I have gotten this houre more shame and harme by thee,

Than all thy life days thou canst do me honestie.

M. Mery. Why, nowe may ye see what it cometh to in the ende,

To make a deadly, foe of your most loving frende:

And, y'wis this letter, if ye woulde heare it now—

C. Custance. I will heare none of it.

M. Mery. In faith, would ravishe you.

C. Custance. He hath stained my name for ever, this is cleare.

R. Royster. I can make all as well in an houre.

M. Mery. (*Aside*.) As ten yeare.

How say ye, wilt ye have him?

C. Custance. No.

M. Mery. Wil ye take him—

C. Custance. I defie him.

M. Mery. At my word?

C. Custance. A shame take him!

Waste no more wynde, for it will never bee!

M. Mery. This one faulte with twaine shall he mended, ye shall see.

Gentle Mistresse Custance now, good Mistresse Custance,

Honey Mistresse Custance now, sweete Mistresse Custance,

Golden Mistresse Custance now, white Mistresse Custance,

Silken Mistresse Custance now, faire Mistresse Custance.

C. Custance. Faith! rather than to mary with suche a doltishe loute,

I woulde matche myselfe with a begger, out of doute.

M. Mery. Then, I can say no more; to speed we are not like,

Except ye rappe out a ragge of your rhetorike

C. Custance. Speak not of winnyng me; for it shall never be so.

R. Royster. Yes, dame, I will have you, whether ye will or no.

I commaunde you to love me! wherfore shoulde ye not?

Is not my love to you chafing and burning hot?

M. Mery. To hir! that is well sayd.

R. Royster. Shall I so breake my braine,[157]

To dote upon you, and ye not love us againe?

M. Mery. Well sayd yet.

C. Custance. Go to, thou goose.

R. Royster. I say, Kit Custance,

In case ye will not haze, well; better yes, perchaunce.

C. Custance. Avaunt, lozell![158] packe thee hence!

M. Mery. Wel sir, ye perceive,

For all your kinde offer, she will not you receive.

R. Royster. Then a strawe for hir, and a strawe for, hir againe;

She shall not be my wife, woulde she never so faine;

No, and though she would be at ten thousande pounde cost.

M. Mery. Lo dame, ye may see what an husbande ye have lost.

C. Custance. Yea, no force;[159] a jewell muche better lost than founde.

M. Mery. Ah, ye will not beleve how this doth my heart wounde.

How shoulde a mariage betwene you be towarde,

If both parties drawe backe, and become so frowarde?

R. Royster. Nay dame, I will fire thee out of thy house, [though I die;]

And destroy thee and all thine, and that by and by.

M. Mery. Nay, for the passion of God, sir, do not so.

R. Royster. Yes, except she will say Yea to that she sayde No.

C. Custance. And what, be there no officers, trowe we, in towne,

To checke idle loytrers, braggyng up and downe?

Where be they, by whome vacabunds shoulde be represt;

That poor sillie widowes might live in peace and rest?

Shall I never ridde thee out of my companie?

I will call for helpe. What hough! come forth Trupenie!

Enter TRUPENIE.

---

[157] *Break my brain.*] So in Lyly's "Maid's Metamorphosis," 1600,—
"In vain, I fear, *I beat my brains about.*" These expressions have the same signification as
the "*Cudgel thy brains no more about it,*" of the *Gravedigger* in "Hamlet."

[158] *Lozell.*] A lozell or losel is a pitiful worthless fellow.

[159] *No force.*] i. e. no matter. It occurs again at p. 201.

Trupenie. Anon. What is your will, Mistresse? Dyd ye call me?

C. Custance. Yea! go, runne apace, and, as fast as may be,
Pray Tristram Trusty, my moste assured frende,
To be here by and by, that he may me defende.

Trupenie. That message so quickly shall be done, by God's grace,
That at my returne ye shall say, I went apace.   [*Exeat.*

C. Custance. Then shall we see, I trowe, whether ye shall do me harme.

R. Royster. Yes, in faith, Kitte, I shall thee and thine so charme,
That all women incarnate by thee may beware.

C. Custance. Nay, as for charming me, come hither if thou dare.
I shall cloute thee tyll thou stinke, both thee and thy traine,
And coyle[160] thee [with] mine owne handes, and sende thee home againe.

R. Royster. Yea, sayst thou me that dame? Dost thou me threaten?
Goe we, I will see whether I shall be beaten.

M. Mery. Nay, for the paishe of God, let me now treate [of] peace;
For, bloudshed will there be, in case this strife increace.
Ah, good dame Custance, take better way with you!

C. Custance. Let him do his worst!

M. Mery. Yeld in time!

R. Royster. Come hence thou!

[*Exeant Royster and Mery.*

ACTUS iiij.   SCÆNA iiij.

CHRISTIAN CUSTANCE — ANOT ALYFACE — TIBET
TALKAPACE — M. MUMBLECRUST.

C. Custance. So, sirra! If I should not with hym take this way,
I shoulde not be ridde of him, I thinke, till doome's day.
I will call forth my folkes, that, without any mockes,
If he come agayne, we may give him rappes and knockes.
Mage Mumblecrust, come forth, and Tibet Talkapace;

---

[160] *Coyle*.] i. e. cuff. In Tim Bobbin's Glossary of the Lancashire Dialect, a *coil* is explained by "a lump raised on the head by a blow."

Yea, and come forth too, Mistresse Annot Alyface.

 An. Alyface. I come.

 Tib. Talk. And I am here.

 M. Mumbl. And I am here too, at length.

 C. Custance. Like warriers, if nede bee, ye must shew your strength.
The man that this day hath thus begiled you
Is Ralph Roister Doister, whome ye knowe well inowe;
The most [doltish] loute and dastarde that ever on grounde trode.

 Tib. Talk. I see all folke mocke hym, when he goth abrode.

 C. Custance. What, pretie maide, will ye talke when I speake?

 Tib. Talk. No, forsooth, good mistresse.

 C. Custance. Will ye my tale breake?—
He threatneth to come hither, with all his force, to fight;
I charge you, if he come, on him with all your might.

 M. Mumbl. I, with my distaffe, will reache him one rappe.

 Tib. Talk. And I, with my newe broome, will sweepe hym one swappe;
And then, with our greate clubbe, I will reache hym one rappe.
And I, with our skimmer, will fling, him one flappe.

 Tib. Talk. Then, Trupenie's fire-fork will him shrewdly fray?
And you, with the spitte, may drive him quite away.

 C. Custance. Goe, make all ready, that it may be e'en so.

 Tib. Talk. For my parte, I 'shrewe them that last about it go.

[Exeant M. Mumbl. Annot, and Tib.

ACTUS iiij. SCÆNA v.

CHRISTIAN CUSTANCE — TRUPENIE — TRISTRAM TRUSTY.

 C. Custance. Trupenie dyd promise me to runne a great pace,
My friend Tristram Trusty to fet into this place.
In deede, he dwelleth hence a good stert, I confesse;
But yet, a quicke messanger might twice since, as I gesse,
Have gone and come againe. Ah, yond I spie him now.

 Trupenie. (*to T. Trusty.*) Ye are a slow goer, sir, I make God a vow;
My Mistresse Custance will in me put all the blame;

Your leggs be longer than myne: come apace, for shame.

    C. Custance. I con[161] thee thanke, Trupenie; thou hast done right wele.

    Trupenie. Maistresse, since I went, no grasse hath growne on my hele;
But, Maister Tristram Trustie here, maketh no speede.

    C. Custance. That he came at all, I thanke him, in very deede;
For, now have I neede of the helpe of some wise man

    T. Trusty. Then may I be gone againe, for none such I am.

    Trupenie. Ye may bee, by your going; for, no alderman
Can goe, I dare say, a sadder pace than ye can.

    C. Custance. Trupenie, get thee in; thou shalt among them knowe,
How to use thyselfe like a propre man, I trowe.

    Trupenie. I go.   [*Ex.*

    C. Custance. Now, Tristram Trusty, I thanke you right much;
For, at my first sending, to come ye never grutch.

    T. Trusty. Dame Custance, God ye save; and, while my life shall last,
For my friende Goodlucke's sake, ye shall not send in wast.

    C. Custance. He shall give you thanks.

    T. Trusty. I will do much for his sake.

    C. Custance. But alack, I feare, great displeasure shall he take.

    T. Trusty. Wherfore?

    C. Custance. For a foolish matter.

    T. Trusty. What is your cause?

    C. Custance. I am yll accombred with a couple of dawes.

    T. Trusty. Nay, weepe not, woman; but tell me what your cause is.
As concerning my friende, is any thing amisse?

    C. Custance. No, not on my part; but, here was Sym Suresby—

    T. Trusty. He was with me, and tolde me so.

    C. Custance. And he stoode by,
While Ralph Roister Doister, with helpe of Merygreeke,
For promise of mariage dyd unto me seeke.

    T. Trusty. And had ye made any promise before, [to] them twaine?

    C. Custance. No, I had rather be torne in pieces, and slaine.
No man hath my faith and trouth, but Gawin Goodlucke,

---

[161] *I con.*] Vide Note 97.

And that, before Suresby dyd I say, and there stucke;
But, of certaine letters there were suche words spoken—

    T. Trusty. He tolde me that too.

    C. Custance. And of a ring and token;
That Suresby, I spied, dyd more than halfe suspect,
That I my faith to Gawyn Goodlucke dyd reject.

    T. Trusty. But was there no suche matter, Dame Custance, in deede?

    C. Custance. If ever my head thought it, God sende me yll speede!
Wherfore, I beseech you, with me to be a witnesse,
That in all my life I never intended thing lesse.
And, what a brainsicke foole Ralph Roister Doister is,
Your selfe know well enough.

    T. Trusty. Ye say full true, y'wis.

    C. Custance. Bicause to be his wife, I ne graunt nor apply,
Hither will be com, he sweareth, by and by,
To kill both me and myne, and beate downe my house flat
Therfore, I pray your aide.

    T. Trusty. I warrant you [for] that.

    C. Custance. Have I so many yeres lived a sobre life,
And shewed myselfe honest, mayde, widowe, and wyfe;
And nowe to be abused in such a vile sorte?
To see howe poore widowes lyve, all voyde of comfort!

    T. Trusty. I warrant hym do you no harme nor wrong at all.

    C. Custance. No, but Mathew Merygreeke doth me most appall;
That he woulde joyne hym selfe with such a wretched loute.

    T. Trusty. He doth it for a jest, I knowe him, out of doubte.
And here cometh Merygreeke?

    C. Custance. Then shal we here his mind.

ACTUS iiij.   SCÆNA vj.

MERYGREEKE — CHRISTIAN CUSTANCE — TRIST.TRUSTY.

    M. Mery. Custance and Trustie both, I doe you here well finde.

    C. Custance. Ah! Mathew Merygreeke, ye have used me well!

M. Mery. Nowe, for altogether,[162] ye must your answere tell.
Will ye have this man, woman? Or else, will ye not?
Else will he come,—never bore so brymme,[163] nor tost so hot.

    Custance. But why joyn ye with him?

    T. Trusty. For mirth?

    C. Custance. Or else in sadnesse?

    M. Mery. The more fond[164] of you both, hardly the mater [to] gesse.

    T. Trusty. Lo, how say ye dame?

    M. Mery. Why, do ye thinke, dame Custance,
That in this wowing I have ment ought but pastance?

    C. Custance. Much things ye spake, I wote, to maintaine his dotage.

    M. Mery. But, well might ye judge, I spake it all in mockage;
For why? Is Roister Doister a fitte husbande for you?

    T. Trusty. I dare say ye never thought it.

    M. Mery. No, to God I vow.
And, dyd not I know afore, of the insurance
Betweene Gawyn Goodlucke and Christian Custance?
And, dyd not I, for the nonce, by my conveyance,
Reade his letter in a wrong sense, for daliance?
That if you coulde have taken it up at the first bounde,
We shoulde therat such a sporte and pastime have founde,
That all the whole towne should have been the merier.

    C. Custance. Ill ake your heades bothe! I was never werier,
Nor never more vexte, since the first day I was borne.

    T. Trusty. But, very well I wist, he here did all in scorne.

    C. Custance. But, I feared therof to take dishonestie.

    M. Mery. This should both have made sporte, and shewed your
        honestie;
And Goodlucke, I dare sweare, your witte therin would 'low.[165]

    T. Trusty. Yea, being no worse than we know it to be now.

---

[162] *Now for altogether.*] i.e. once for all.

[163] *Never bore so brymme.*] i. e. so fierce. A sow is said *to go to brim*, when she is ready to take the boar.

[164] *Fond.*] Dull—silly.

[165] *'Low.*] i. e. allow.

M. Mery. And nothing yet to late; for, when I come to him,
Hither will he repaire with a sheepe's looke full grim,
By plaine force and violence, to drive you to yelde.
   C. Custance. If ye two bidde me, we will with him pitche a fielde,
I and my maides together.
   M. Mery. Let us see; be bolde!
   C. Custance. Ye shall see womens' warre.
   T. Trusty. That fight will I beholde.
   M. Mery. If occasion serve, takyng his parte full brim,
I will strike at you, but the rappe shall lighten him.
When we first appeare——
   C. Custance. Then will I runne away,
As though I were afearde.
   T. Trusty. Do you that part wel play,
And I will sue for peace.
   M. Mery. And I will set him on;
Then will he looke as fierce as a Cotssold lyon.[166]
   T. Trusty. But, when go'st thou for him?
   M. Mery. That do I very nowe.
   C. Custance. Ye shal finde us here.
   M. Mery. Wel, God have mercy on you.   *Ex.*
   T. Trusty. There is no cause of feare; the least boy in the streete——
   C. Custance. Nay, the least girle I have, will make him take his feete.
But hearke, me thinke they make preparation.
   T. Trusty. No force, it will be a good recreation.
   C. Custance. I will stande within, and steppe forth speedily,
And so make as though I ranne away dreadfully.   [*Ex.*

---

[166] *A Cotssold lyon.*] A sheep. Cotswold (pronounced cotsold) is an old word for a sheepcote. Hence, certain hills in Gloucestershire, famous for the pasturage of sheep, acquired the name of Cotswold Hills.

ACTUS iiij.   SCÆNA vij.

RALPH ROYSTER — M. MERYGREEKE — D. DOUGHTIE —
HARPAX — TRISTRAM TRUSTY.

R. Royster. Nowe Sirs, keepe your 'ray, and see your heartes be stoute.
But, where be these caitifes? Me think they dare not route.[167]
How say'st thou, Merygreeke? What doth Kit Custance say?
M. Mery. I am loth to tell you.
R. Royster. Tushe, speake man. Yea or nay?
M. Mery. Forsooth sir, I have spoken for you all that I can;
But, if ye winne hir, ye must e'en play the man;
E'en to fight it out, ye must a man's heart take.
R. Royster. Yes, they shall know, and thou knowest, I have a stomacke.
M. Mery. A. stomacke (quod you) yea, as good as ere man had.
R. Royster. I trowe, they shall finde and feele that I am a lad.
M. Mery. By this crosse, I have seene you eate your meate as well
As any that ere I have seene of, or heard tell.
A stomacke, quod you! He that will that denie,
I know, was never at dynner in your companie.
R. Royster. Nay, the stomacke of a man it is that I meane.
M. Mery. Nay, the stomacke of an horse or a dogge, I weene.
R. Royster. Nay, a man's stomacke with a weapon, meane I.
M. Mery. Ten men can scarce match you with a spoone in a pie.
R. Royster. Nay, the stomacke of a man to trie in strife.
M. Mery. I never saw your stomacke cloyde yet in my lyfe.
R. Royster. Tushe, I meane in strife or fighting to trie.
M. Mery. We shall see how ye will strike nowe, being angry.
R. Royster. Have at thy pate then, and save thy head if thou may.
M. Mery. Nay then, have at your pate agayne, by this day.
R. Royster. Nay, thou may'st not strike at me againe, in no wise.

---

[167] *Route.*] This verb, which is not of common occurrence, means to *assemble*. It is used
by Bacon, in his "History of Henry the Seventh," p. 68, fol. 1629, where, speaking of the Earl
of Northumberland, who was slain by the populace, while levying taxes in Yorkshire, he says,
"The meaner sort *routed* together, and suddenly, assayling the Earle in his house, slew him."

202

M. Mery. I can not in fight, make to you suche warrantise:
But, as for your foes here, let them the bargaine 'bie.[168]
   R. Royster. Nay as for [them] they shall every mother's childe die.
And, in this my fume, a little thing might make me
To beate downe house and all; and else, the devill take me.
   M. Mery. If I were as ye be, by Gog's deare mother,
I woulde not leave one stone upon another.
Though she woulde redeeme it with twentie thousand poundes.
   R. Royster. It shall be even so, by his lily woundes!
   M. Mery. Bee not at one with hir,[169] upon any amendes.
   R. Royster. No, though she make to me never so many frendes.
Not if all the worlde for hir woulde undertake.
No, not God himselfe neither, shall not hir peace make.
On, therfore; marche forwarde. Soft, stay a whyle yet.
   M. Mery. On.
   R. Royster. Tary.
   M. Mery. On.
   R. Royster. Soft. Now forward sett.

Enter C. CUSTANCE.

C. Custance. What businesse have we here? Out, alas, alas!

[*Runs out.*

   R. Royster. Ha, ha, ha, ha, ha!
Dydst thou see that, Merygreeke, howe afrayde she was?
Dydst thou see howe she fledde apace out of my sight?
Ah, good sweete Custance, I pitie hir, by this light.
   M. Mery. That tender heart of yours wyll marre altogether;
Thus will ye be turned with waggyng of a fether.
   R. Royster. On sirs, keepe your 'ray.
   M. Mery. On forth, while this geare is hot.

---

[168] *'Bie.*] i. e. aby, *viz.* abide.
"Nought that wanteth rest can long *aby.*"
"*Faerie Queene,*" Book 3, Canto 7.
[169] *Bee not at one with hir.*] i. e. Be not reconciled. *At one* is used in this sense by Jonson
and others.

203

R. Royster. Soft, [by] the Armes of Caleys, I have one thing forgot.

M. Mery. What lacke we now?

R. Royster. Retire, or else we be all slain.

M. Mery. Backe, for the pashe of God; backe, sirs, backe againe![170]
What is the great mater?

R. Royster. This hastie forth goyng

  Had almost brought us all to utter undoing;

  It made me forget a thing most necessarie.

M. Mery. Well remembred of a captaine, by Sainct Marie.

R. Royster. It is a thing must be had.

M. Mery. Let us have it then.

R. Royster. But I wote not where nor how.

M. Mery. Then wote not I when.
But what is it?

R. Royster. Of a chiefe thing I am to seeke.

M. Mery. Tut, so will ye be, when ye have studied a weke.
But, tell me what it is.

R. Royster. I lacke yet an hedpiece.

M. Mery. The kitchen collocavit's the best, hennes to Grece;
Runne, fet it Dobinet, and come at once withall,
And bryng with thee my potgunne,[171] hangyng by the wall.

> [*Ex. D. Doughtie.*

I have seene your head with it, full many a tyme,
Covered as safe as it had bene with a skrine:
And, I warrant it save your head from any stroke,
Except perchaunce to be amased with the smoke:
I warrant your head therwith, except for the mist,
As safe as if it were locked up in a chist.
And loe, here our Dobinet commeth with it nowe.

------

[170] This line, I think, belongs to *R. Royster*.
"Pashe" is an abbreviation of *passion*.

[171] *Potgunne.*] A small gun—a corruption of popgun.
"I hope to see the boys make *Potguns* of thee."
"Scornful Lady," Act 5, Scene 1.

Re-enter D. DOUGHTIE.

D. Dough. It will cover me to the shoulders well inow.

M. Mery. Let me see it on.

R. Royster. In fayth it doth metely well.

M. Mery. There can be no fitter thing. Now ye must us tell
What to do.

R. Royster. Now forth in 'ray, sirs, and stoppe no more,

M. Mery. Now, Sainct George to borow. Drum, dubbe a dubbe afore!

T. Trusty. What meane you to do, Sir? Committee manslaughter?

R. Royster. To kyll fortie such, is a matter of laughter.

T. Trusty. And who is it, Sir, whome ye intende thus to spill?

R. Royster. Foolishe Custance here forceth me against my will.

T. Trusty. And is there no meane, your extreme wrath to slake?
She shall some amendes unto your good mashyp make.

R. Royster. I will none amendes.

T. Trusty. Is hir offence so sore?

M. Mery. And he were a loute, she coulde have done no more.
She hath calde him foole, and 'dressed him like a foole,
Mocked him lyke a foole, used him like a foole.

T. Trusty. Well, yet the sheriffe, the justice, or constable,
Hir misdemeanour to punishe might be able.

R. Royster. No, sir; I mine owne selfe will, in this present cause,
Be sheriffe, and justice, and whole judge of the lawes.
This matter to amende, all officers be I shall:
Constable, bailiffe, sergeant—

M. Mery. And hangman and all.

T. Trusty. Yet, a noble courage, and the hearte of a man,
Should more honour winne by bearyng with a woman.
Therfore, take the lawe, and let hir answere therto.

R. Royster. Merygreeke, the best way were even so to do.
What honour should it be with a woman to fight?

M. Mery. And what, then, will ye thus forgo and lose your right?[172]

R. Royster. Nay, I will take the lawe on hir, withouten grace.

---

[172] *Lese your right.*] Our old writers generally use leese for lose.

205

T. Trusty. Or, yf your mashyp coulde pardon this one trespace,
I pray, you, forgive hir.

R. Royster. Hoh!

M. Mery. Tushe, tushe, sir, do not.

T. Trusty. Be good maister to hir.

R. Royster. Hoh!

M. Mery. Tushe, I say, do not.

T. Trusty. And what, shall your people here, returne streight home?

R. Royster. Yea, levie the campe, sirs; and hence againe, eche one.
But, be still in readinesse, if I happe to call;
I can not tell what sodaine chaunce may befall.

M. Mery. Do not off your harnesse sirs, I you advise,
At the least for this fortnight, in no manner wise.
Perchaunce, in an houre, when all ye thinke least,
Our maister's appetite to fight will be best.
But soft, ere ye go, have once at Custance' house.

R. Royster. Soft, what wilt thou do?

M. Mery. Once discharge my harquebouse;
And, for my hearte's ease, have once more with my potgoon.

R. Royster. Hold thy handes! else is all our purpose cleane fordoone.

M. Mery. And it cost me my life.

R. Royster. I say, thou shalt not.

M. Mery. By the masse, but I will have once more with haile shot.
I wil have some penyworth, I will not leese all.

ACTUS iiij.   SCÆNA viij.

M. MERYGREEKE — C. CUSTANCE — T. TRUSTY — R. ROYSTER — TIB. TALK. — AN. ALYFACE — M. MUMBLECRUST — TRUPENIE — DOBINETDOUGHTIE — HARPAX.

Two Drummes with their Ensignes.

C. Custance. What caitifes are those, that so shake my house wall?

M. Mery. Ah sirrha[173] now, Custance, if ye had so muche wit,

---

[173] *Sirrha.*] Vide Note 102.

I would see you aske pardon, and your selves submit.

    C. Custance. Have I still this adoe with a couple of fooles?

    M. Mery. Here ye what she saith?

    C. Custance. Maidens, come forth with your tooles,

In array.

    M. Mery. Dubba dub, sirrha!

    R. Royster. In array

They come sodainly on us.

    M. Mery. Dubbadub!

    R. Royster. In array.

That ever I was borne, we are taken tardie!

    M. Mery. Now sirs, 'quite your selves like tall men and hardie.

    C. Custance. On afore, Trupenie! Holde thyne owne, Annot!

On towarde them, Tibet, for scape us they can not!

Come forth, Madge Mumblecrust! so, stande fast togither.

    M. Mery. God, sende us a faire day!

    R. Royster. See, they marche on hither.

    Tib. Talk. But, mistresse.

    C. Custance. What say'st thou?

    Tib. Talk. Shall I go fet our goose?

    C. Custance. What to do?

    Tib. Talk. To yonder captain I will turne hir loose.

And she gape and hisse at him, as she doth at me,

I durst jeoparde my hande she wyll make him flee.

    C. Custance. On forward!

    R. Royster. They com.

    M. Mery. Stand!

    R. Royster. Hold!

    M. Mery. Kepe!

    R. Royster. There!

    M. Mery. Strike!

    R. Royster. Take heede!

    C. Custance. Well sayd, Trupeny!

    Trupeny. Ah, whooresons!

    C. Custance. Well don, in deede!

M. Mery. Holde thine owne, Harpax! Downe with them, Dobinet!

C. Custance. Now, Madge; there, Annot; now sticke them, Tibet!

Tib. Talk. All my chiefe quarrell is to this same little knave,
That begyled me last day; nothyng shall him save.

D. Dough. Downe with this little queane, that hath at me such spite;
Save you from hir, maister, it is a very sprite.

C. Custance. I myselfe will mounsire graund captaine undertake.

R. Royster. They win grounde!

M. Mery. Save your selfe, sir, for God's sake!

R. Royster. Out, alas, I am slaine; helpe!

M. Mery. Save your selfe!

R. Royster. Alas!

M. Mery. Nay then, have at you mistresse!

R. Royster. Thou hittest me, alas!

M. Mery. I wil strike at Custance here.

R. Royster. Thou hittest me!

M. Mery. So I will. (*Aside.*)
Nay, mistresse Custance.

R. Royster. Alas, thou hittest me still!
Hold!

M. Mery. Save your selfe sir!

R. Royster. Help, out alas, I am slain!

M. Mery. Truce, hold your hands; truce, for a pissing while[174] or twaine:
Now, how say you, Custance, for saving of your life,
Will ye yelde, and graunt to be this gentleman's wife?

C. Custance. He tolde me he loved me; call ye this love?

M. Mery. He loved [ye] a while, even like a turtle dove.

C. Custance. Gay love, God save it; so soon hotte, so soone colde.

M. Mery. I am sory for you: he coulde love you yet, so he coulde.

R. Royster. Nay, by Cook's precious, she shall be none of mine.

M. Mery. Why so?

---

[174] *A passing while.*] i. e. a short time.—"He had not been there but *a passing while*, but all the chamber smelled him."—"*Two Gentlemen of Verona*," Act 4, Scene 4.

R. Royster. Come away, by the masse she is mankine.[175]
I durst adventure the losse of my right hande,
If she dyd not slee hir other husbande.
And see, if she prepare not againe to fight.
 M. Mery. What then? Sainct George to borow, our ladie's knight.
 R. Royster. Slee else whom she will; by Gog, she shall not slee mee.
 M. Mery. How then?
 R. Royster. Rather than to be slaine, I will flee.
 C. Custance. Too it againe, my knightesses; downe with them all!
 R. Royster. Away, away, away, she will else kyll us all!
 M. Mery. Nay, sticke to it, like an hardie man and a tall.
 R. Royster. Oh, bones, thou hittest me! Away, or else die we shall.
 M. Mery. Away, for the pashe ef our sweete Lord Jesus Christ.
 C. Custance. Away, loute and lubber, or I shall be thy priest!
So, this fielde is ours; we have driven them all away.
        [Exeant Ralph. Mat. Dob. and Harpax.
 Tib. Talk. Thankes to God, mistresse, ye have had a faire day.
 C. Custance. Well, nowe goe ye in, and make your selfe some good cheere.
 Omnes Pariter. We goe.
 T. Trusty. Ah sir, what a field we have had heere.
 C. Custance. Friend Tristram, I pray you be a witnesse with me.
 T. Trusty. Dame Custance, I shall depose for your honestie. .
And nowe, fare ye well, except some thing else ye wolde.
 C. Custance. Not now, but when I nede to sende, I will be bolde.
I thanke you for these paines. And now I wyll get me in;
Now Roister Doister will no more wowyng begin.   *[Ex.*

ACTUS v. SCÆNA j.

GAWYN GOODLUCKE — SYM. SURESBY.

 G. Good. Sym. Suresby, my trustie man, nowe advise thee well,
And see that no false surmises thou me tell;

---

[175] *She is mankine.*] Mankind is used by Shakspeare and other writers as an adjective, in
the sense of masculine—ferocious—sanguinary.

Was there such adoe about Custance, of a truth?

 Sym. Sure. To reporte that I hearde and sawe, to me is ruth;
But, both my duetie, and name, and propretie,
Warneth me to you to shewe fidelitie.
It may be well enough, and I wishe it so to be,
She may hir selfe discharge, and trie hir honestie;
Yet, their clayme to hir, me thought, was very large,
For, with letters, rings, and tokens, they dyd hir charge.
Which when I hearde and sawe, I would none to you bring.

 G. Good. No, by Sainct Marie, I allowe thee[176] in that thing.
Ah, sirrha, nowe I see truthe in the proverbe olde,
All things that shineth, is not by and by pure golde:
If any doe lyve a woman of honestie,
I would have sworne Christian Custance had bene shee.

 Sym. Sure. Sir, though I to you be a servant true and just,
Yet, doe not ye therfore your faithfull spouse mystrust.
But, examine the matter, and if ye shall it finde
To be all well, be not for my wordes unkinde.

 G. Good. I shall do that is right, and as I see cause why.
But, here commeth Custance forth; we shal know by and by.

ACTUS v.   SCÆNA ij.

C. CUSTANCE — GAWYN GOODLUCKE — SYM. SURESBY.

 C. Custance. I come forth to see and hearken for newes good;
For, about this houre is the tyme, of likelyhood,
That Gawyn Goodlucke, by the sayings of Suresby,
Woulde be at home; and lo, yond I see hym I.
What, Gawyn Goodlucke, the onely hope of my life,
Welcome home, and kysse me, your true espoused wife.

---

[176] *I allowe thee*] i. e. I approve of your conduct.
   "I like them all, and do *approve* them all."
      "Henry IV. Part 2," Act 4, Scene 2.

G. Good. Nay, soft, dame Custance, I must first, by your licence,
See whether all things be cleere in your conscience;
I heare of your doings to me very straunge.

    C. Custance. What! feare ye that my faith towardes you shoulde change?

    G. Good. I must needes mistrust ye be elsewhere entangled,
For I heare that certaine men with you have wrangled
About the promise of mariage by you to them made.

    C. Custance. Coulde any man's reporte youre minde therein persuade?

    G. Good. Well, ye must therin declare your selfe to stande cleere,
Else, I and you, dame Custance, may not joyne this yere.

    C. Custance. Then woulde I were dead, and faire layd in my grave.
Ah! I, Suresby, is this the honestie that ye have,
To hurt me with your report, not knowyng the thing?

    Sym. Sure. If ye be honest, my wordes can hurte you nothing.
But, what I hearde and sawe, I might not but report.

    C. Custance. Ah! Lorde, helpe poore widowes, destitute of comfort.
Truly, most deare spouse, nought was done but for pastance.

    G. Good. But, such kynde of sporting, is homely daliance.

    C. Custance. If ye knewe the truthe, ye would take all in good parte.

    G. Good. By your leave, I am not halfe well skilled in that arte.

    C. Custance. It was none but Roister Doister, that foolishe mome.

    G. Good. Yea, Custance, better (they say) a badde 'scuse, than none.

    C. Custance. Why, Tristram Trustie, sir, your true and faithfull frende,
Was privie bothe to the beginning and the ende.
Let him be the judge, and for me testifie.

    G. Good. I will the more credite that he shall verifie;
And, bicause I will the truthe know, e'en as it is,
I will to hym my selfe, and know all, without misse.
Come on, Sym Suresby, that before my friend thou may
Avouch thee the same wordes, which thou dydst to me say.

[Exeunt G. Good. and Sym Sure.

211

ACTUS v.   SCÆNA iij.

CHRISTIAN CUSTANCE.

C. Custance. O Lorde, howe necessarie it is nowe of dayes,
That eche bodie live uprightly all maner [of] wayes;
For, lette never so little a gappe be open,
And be sure of this, the worst shall be spoken.
Howe innocent stande I in this for deede or thought!
And yet, see what mistrust towardes me it hath wrought.
But thou, Lorde, knowest all folkes' thoughts, and eke intents;
And thou arte the deliverer of all innocentes.
Thou didst helpe the advoutresse,[177] that she might be amended;
Much more then helpe [me,] Lorde, that never yll intended.
Thou didst helpe Susanna, wrongfully accused,
And no lesse dost thou see, Lorde, how I am now abused.
Thou didst helpe Hester, when she should have died;
Helpe [me] also, good Lorde, that my truth may be tried.
Yet, if Gawyn Goodlucke with Tristram Trustie speake,
I trust of yll report the force shall be but weake;
And loe, yond' they come, sadly talking together;
I wyll abyde, and not shrink for their comming hither.

ACTUS v.   SCÆNA iiij.

GAWYN GOODLUCKE — TRISTRAM TRUSTY — C. CUSTANCE — SYM. SURESBY.

G. Good. And was it none other than ye to me reporte?
T. Trusty. No; and here were ye wished, to have seene the sporte.
G. Good. Woulde I had, rather than halfe of that in my purse.
Sym. Sure. And I doe much rejoice the matter was no worse.

---

[177] *Advoutresse.*] i. e. adult'ress. In Cartwright's "Ordinary," Act 4, Scene 5, the *Constable* says, "I'll look there shall be no *advoutry* in my ward."

And, like as to open it I was to you faithfull,
So of Dame Custance' honest truth I am joyful.
For, God forfende that I should hurt hir by false reporte.

    G. Good. Well, I will no longer holde hir in discomforte.

    C. Custance. Nowe come they hitherwarde, I trust all shall be well.

    G. Good. Sweete Custance, neither heart can thinke, nor tongue tell,
Howe muche I joy in your constant fidelitie.
Com nowe, kisse me, the pearle of perfect honestie.

    C. Custance. God lette me no longer to continue in lyfe,
Than I shall towardes you continue a true wyfe.

    G. Good. Well, now to make you for this some parte of amendes,
I shall desire first you, and then suche of our frendes,
As shall to you seeme best, to suppe at home with me,
Where at your fought fielde we shall laugh and mery be.

    Sym. Sure. And, mistresse, I beseech you, take with me no greefe:[178]
I did a true man's part, not wishyng you repreefe.

    C. Custance. Though hastie reportes, through surmises growying,
May of poore innocentes be utter overthrowyng,
Yet, bicause to thy maister thou hast a true hart,
And I know mine owne truth, I forgive thee, for my part.

    G. Good. Go we all to my house, and of this geare no more.
Goe, prepare all things, Sym. Suresby; hence, runne afore!

    Sym. Sure. I goe.   [*Ex.*

    G. Good. Good. But who commeth yond? M. Merygreeke?

    C. Custance. Roister Doister's champion; I 'shrewe his best cheeke.

    T. Trusty. Roister Doister's selfe, your wower, is with hym too.
Surely, some thing there is with us they have to doe.

---

[178] *Take with me no greefe.*] Bear me no ill-will.

ACTUS v.   SCÆNA v.

M. MERYGREEKE — RALPH ROYSTER — G. GOODLUCKE —
TRISTRAM TRUSTY — C. CUSTANCE.

M. Mery. (*To Ralph.*) Yond' I see Gawyn Goodlucke, to whome lyeth
　　my message,
I wyll first salute him after his long voyage,
And then make all things well concerning your behalfe.
　　R. Royster. Yea, for the pashe of God.
　　M. Mery. Hence, out of sight, ye calfe,
Till I have spoke with them, and then I will you fet.
　　R. Royster. In God's name.　　　　　　　　　　　　　　　　　[*Ex.*
　　M. Mery. What, master Gawyn Goodlucke, wel met;
And, from your long voyage, I bid you right welcome home.
　　G. Good. I thanke you.
　　M. Mery. I come to you from an honest mome.
　　G. Good. Who is that?
　　M. Mery. Roister Doister, that doughtie kite.
　　C. Custance. Fye, I can scarce abide ye shoulde his name recite.
　　M. Mery. Ye must take him to favour, and pardon all [that's] past;
He heareth of your returne, and is full yll agast.
　　G. Good. I am ryght well content, he have with us some chere.
　　C. Custance. Fye upon him, beast; then wyll not I be there.
　　G. Good. Why, Custance, doe ye hate hym more than ye love me?
　　C. Custance. But for your mynde sir, where he were, would I not be.
　　T. Trusty. He woulde make us all laugh.
　　M. Mery. Ye nere had better sport.
　　G. Good. I pray you, sweete Custance, let him to us resort.
　　C. Custance. To your will I assent.
　　M. Mery. Why, suche a foole it is,
As no man for good pastime would forgoe or misse.
　　G. Good. Fet him, to go wyth us.
　　M. Mery. He will be a glad man.　　　　　　　　　　　　　　[*Ex.*

T. Trusty. We must, to make us mirth, maintaine hym[179] all we can.
And loe, yond' he commeth, and Merygreeke with him.

C. Custance. At his first entrance, ye shall see I wyll him trim.
But first, let us hearken the gentleman's wise talke.

T. Trusty. I pray you, marke if ever ye sawe crane so stalke.

ACTUS v.   SCÆNA vj.

R. ROISTER — M. MERYGREEKE — C. CUSTANCE — G. GOODLUCKE — T. TRUSTY.

R. Royster. May I then be bolde?

M. Mery. I warrant you on my worde;
They say they shall be sicke, but ye be at their borde.

R. Royster. They were not angry then?

M. Mery. Yes, at first, and made strange;
But, when I sayd your anger to favour shoulde change,
And therewith had commended you accordingly,
They were all in love with your mashyp by and by.
And cried you mercy, that they had done you wrong.

R. Royster. For why, no man, woman, nor childe can hate me long.

M. Mery. We feare (quod they) be will be avenged one day;
Then for a peny give all our lives we may.

R. Royster. Sayd they so in deede?

M. Mery. Did they? yea, even with one voice.
He will forgive all (quod I.) Oh, how they did rejoice!

R. Royster. Ha, ha, ha!

M. Mery. Gee fette hym (say they) while he is in good moode;
For, have his anger who lust, we will not by the roode.

R. Royster. I pray God that it be all true, that thou hast me tolde,
And that she fight no more.

---

[179] *Maintaine hym*] i. e. encourage him. So in the Epistle to Gabriel Hervey, prefixed to Spenser's "Shepherd's Calendar:"—"The Right Worshipfull Maister Philip Sidney, is a speciall favourer and *maintainer* of all kinde of learning."

M. Mery. I warrant you, be bolde.
To them, and salute them.

   R. Royster. Sirs, I greete you all well.

   Omnes. Your maistership is welcom.

   C. Custance. Savyng my quarell.
For sure I will put you up into the Eschequer.

   M. Mery. Why so? Better nay. Wherfore?

   C. Custance. For an usurer.

   R. Royster. I am no usurer, good mistresse, by his armes.

   M. Mery. When tooke he gaine of money, to any man's harmes?

   C. Custance. Yes, a fowle, usurer he is, ye shall see els.

   R. Royster. (Aside to M. Mery.) Did'st not thou promise she would picke
      no mo quarels?

   C. Custance. He will lende no blowes, but he have in recompense.
Fiftene for one, which is to muche of conscience.

   R. Royster. Ah dame, by the auncient lawe of armes, a man
Hath no honour to foile his handes on a woman.

   C. Custance. And where other usurers take their gaines yerely,
This man is angry, but he have his by and by.

   G. Good. Sir, doe not for hir sake beare me your displeasure.

   M. Mery. Well, he shall with you talke therof more at leasure.
Upon your good usage, he will now shake your hande.

   R. Royster. And muche heartily welcome from a straunge lande.

   M. Mery. Be not afearde, Gawyn, to let him shake your fyst.

   G. Good. Oh, the moste honeste gentleman that ere I wist.
I beseeche your mashyp to take payne to suppe with us.

   M. Mery. He shall not say you nay; (and I too, by Jesus;)
Bicause ye shall be friends, and let all quarels passe.

   R. Royster. I wyll be as good friends with them as ere I was.

   M. Mery. Then, let me fet your quier, that we may have a song.

   R. Royster. Goe.   *[Ex. M. Mery.*

   G. Good. I have hearde no melodie all this yeare long.

   Re-enter M. MERY, *with* D. DOUGHTIE *and* HARPAX.

   M. Mery. Come on, sirs, quickly.

R. Royster. Sing on, sirs, for my frends' sake.

D. Dough. Cal ye these your frends?

R. Royster. Sing on, and no mo words make.

Here they sing.

G. Good. The Lord preserve our most noble Queene of renowne,
And hir vertues rewarde with the heavenly crowne.

C. Custance. The Lorde strengthen hir most excellent Majestie,
Long to reigne over us in all prosperitie.

T. Trusty. That hir godly proceedings, the faith to defende,
He may 'stablishe and maintaine to the ende.

M. Mery. God graunt hir, as she doth, the Gospell to protect,
Learning and vertue to advaunce, and vice to correct!

R. Royster. God graunt hir lovyng subjects, both the minde and grace,
Hir most godly proceedings worthily to imbrace.

Harpax. Hir highnesse' most worthy counsellers, God prosper,
With honour and love of all men to minister.

Omnes. God graunt the nobilitie hir to serve and love,
With all the whole commontie, as doth them behove!

AMEN![180]

---

[180] In the infancy of our Drama, the custom of concluding Plays with a prayer of this kind, was very common. Several instances of it are collected in the notes on "Henry IV. part 2," in the *Var. Edit.* of Shakspeare. Steevens surmises that hence originated the practice, till very recently observed, of appending the words *Vivant Rex et Regina* to the Play-bills.

Certaine Songs, to be song by those which use this Comedie or Enterlude.

(Referred to at p. 160)

Who so to marry a minion wyfe,[181]
    Hath hadde good chaunce and happe,
Must love hir and cherishe hir all his life,
    And dandle hir in his lappe.

If she will fare well, yf she wyll go gay,
    A good husbande ever styll,
(What ever she lust to doe or to say,)
    Must lette hir have hir owne will.

About what affaires so ever he goe,
    He must shewe hir all his mynde,
None of hys counsell she may be kept froe,
    Else is he a man unkynde.

(Referred to at p. 180)

I mun be maried a Sunday;
I mun be waried a Sunday;
Who soever shall come that way,
I mun be waried a Sunday.

Roister Doister is my name;
Roister Doister is my name;
A lustie brute I am the same;
I mun be maried a Sunday;

Christian Custance have I founde;
Christian Custance have I founde;

---

[181] *A minion wyfe.*] i. e. A gay, dressy, accomplished wife.

A Widowe worthe a thousande pounde:—
I mun be waried a Sunday.

Custance is as sweete as honey;
Custance is as sweete as honey;
I hir lambe, and she my coney;—
I mun be maried a Sunday.

When we shall make our weddyng feast,
When we shall make our weddyng feast,
There shall bee cheere for man and beast;
I mun be married a Sunday.

      I mun be maried a Sunday, &c.

THE PSALMODIE. (*Vide p. 176*)

Placebo dilexi.
I Maister Roister Doister will streight go home and die,
Our Lorde Jesus Christ his soule have mercie upon:
Thus you see to day a man, to morrow John.

Yet, saving for a woman's extreeme crueltie,
He might have lyved yet a moneth, or two, or three;
But, in spite of Custance, which hath him weried,
His mashyp shall be worshipfully buried.
And, while some piece of his soule is yet hym within,
Some parte of his funeralls let us here beginne.
Durige. He will go darklyng to his grave.
Neque lux, neque crux, nisi solum clinke,
Never gentleman so went to ward heaven, I thinke.

Yet, sirs, as ye wyll the blisse of heaven win,
When he commeth to the grave, lay hym softly in;
And all men take heede by this one gentleman,
Howe you sette your love upon an unkinde woman;

For, these women be all suche madde pievishe elves,
They will not be wonne, except it please themselves.
But, in faith Custance, if ever ye come in hell,
Maister Roister Doister shall serve you as well.

(*Vide p. 177*)

Good night, Roger olde knave; Farewell, Roger olde knave;
Good night, Roger olde knave; knave knap.
Nequaudo. Audivi vocem. Requiem æternam.

The Peale of belles, rong by the Parish Clerk,
and Roister Doister's foure men.

(*Vide p. 183*)

The first Bell, a Triple.—When dyed he? When dyed he?
The seconde.—We have hym! We have hym!
The thirde.—Roister Doister! Roister Doister!
The Fourth Bell.—He commeth! He commeth!
The greate Bell.—Our owne! Our owne!

FINIS.

www.ingramcontent.com/pod-product-compliance
Lightning Source LLC
Chambersburg PA
CBHW051920110726
47902CB00002B/358